Key Stage 3
English
Ages 11–12

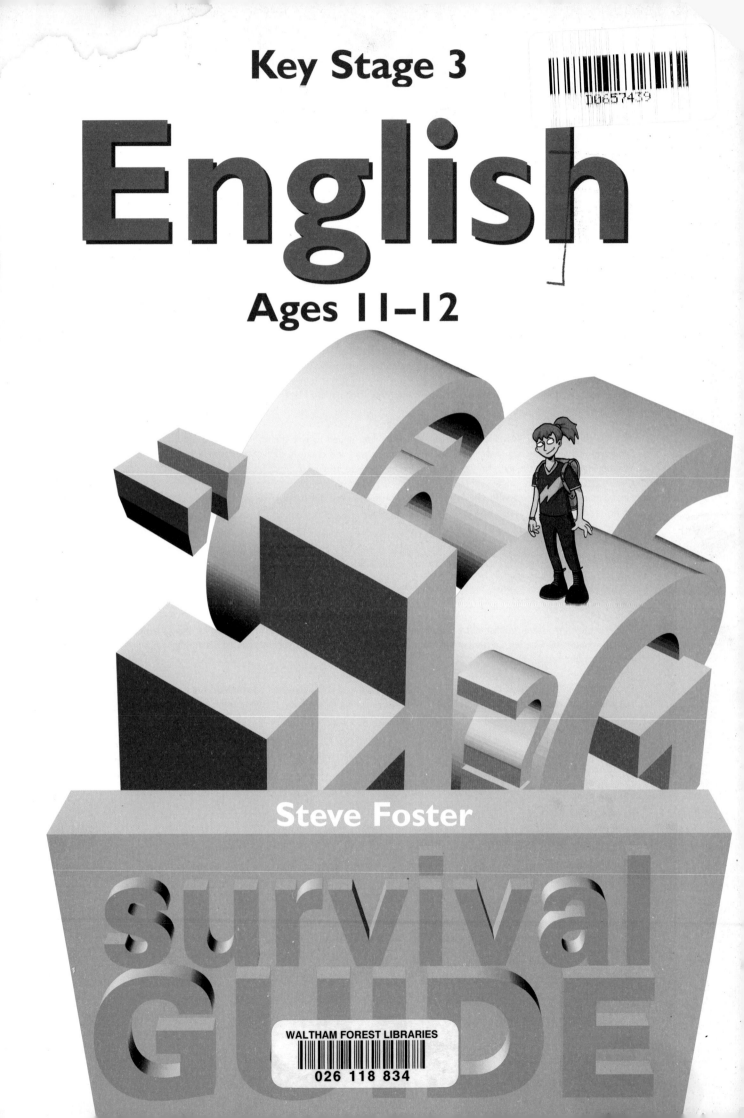

Steve Foster

survival GUIDE

For my brother, Richard

References

Key Stage 3 Literacy Guidelines (2000), Hampshire Inspection and Advisory Service
Literacy Strategies (draft) (2000), Qualifications and Curriculum Authority
Literacy Strategies (2001), Qualifications and Curriculum Authority (website)

I am grateful to John Baxter, John and Judith Polley, John Scicluna and Margaret Veale – many of whose ideas are represented here.

Work with primary pupils in Hampshire and Wiltshire has helped to give me an insight into the Literacy Programme. I am especially grateful to the Headteacher, staff and children of Wallop Junior School, Nether Wallop, Hampshire – the experience gained there has proved invaluable.

Finally, many thanks to my wife, Gill, who has been both tolerant and supportive during the writing of this book - and given me practical advice and help at the end.

Acknowledgements

The author and publisher are grateful to the copyright holders, as credited, for permission to use quoted materials and photographs.

Cider with Rosie by Laurie Lee, published by Hogarth Press. Reprinted by permission of The Random House Group Ltd.
Warning by Jenny Joseph, published by Bloodaxe. Reprinted by permission of John Johnson Literary Agency.
Timothy Winters by Charles Causley, published by Macmillan. Reprinted by permission of David Higham Associates Limited.

Every effort has been made to trace the copyright holders and to obtain their permission for the use of copyright material. The author and publisher will gladly receive information enabling them to rectify any error or omission in subsequent editions.

Letts Educational
Chiswick Centre
414 Chiswick High Road
London W4 5TF
Tel: 020 8996 3333
Fax: 020 8742 8390
Email: *mail@lettsed.co.uk*
Website: *www.letts-education.com*

First published 2001
Reprinted 2002

Text © Steve Foster 2001

British Library Cataloging in Publication Data. A CIP record of this book is available from the British Library.

ISBN 1 84085 633 5

Letts Educational Limited is a division of Granada Learning Limited, part of the Granada Media Group.

Edited and typeset by Cambridge Publishing Management
Designed by Moondisks Limited

English
Book 1 Ages 11-12

Introduction .5

Each unit in this book is targeted at one of the following areas of the KS 3 Literacy Framework: Word level (W), Sentence level (S), Text level – Reading (TR) or Text level – Writing (TW).

Introduction

If you follow a few simple guidelines, this book will help you with your English work in Year 7. Some of the topics may be new to you and others you may have met before. After glancing at some of the pages you feel a little worried. There are sure to be subjects, words and vocabulary which are all strange and new. Do not be alarmed, you are not expected to know all about these things straight away! Whatever you do, do not try to read the whole book at once. Instead, follow these three points:

- **Get to know the book.** Look through the book so that you know what is in it. Take time to read through the Contents page. Browse through the main sections – they are arranged in Word, Sentence and Text levels just like your work at primary school.

- **What is helpful now?** Having had a careful look at the topics in the book, which ones would be most useful to you at the moment? The units on Homework and presentation, Handwriting and Spelling strategies might make a good starting point. Are there any topics where your memory is a bit rusty? Use the book to help you revise things you have learnt but since forgotten.

- **What will be helpful later?** There are units to help and support you both in class and at home. If you have difficulty with work which you are doing during lessons then look up the topic in the Contents and Index sections. The Jargonbuster (Glossary) may also be useful. There is certain to be information on most of the tasks you will be set. For a homework task, there will be several units which can help you. For example, if you are writing a story you will find advice on vocabulary, how to describe people and places, how to plan, draft and present your work.

Singulars and plurals

Things which are found on their own (singly) are called singulars. When there is more than one of them they are called plurals. Often a singular can be changed to a plural by adding *s*.
At other times the endings can be more difficult:

Example

boy becomes *boys*

Example
wolf
wolves

hippopotamus
hippopotamuses

goose
geese

baby
babies

sheep
sheep

Exercise 1

Make these singulars into plurals.

knife-knives fly deer calf half woman stadium
octopus radius

Check your answers in a dictionary.

Exercise 2

Think of five rules which would teach someone how to change singular words into plurals.

1. If a word ends in -*y* drop the *y* and add -*ies*.

RED ALERT Think about what rule you are using to change from singular to plural. **ALER**

Wordfinder

You will already know many words from the English language. Some may be short words of only one or two letters and, perhaps, only one syllable – others may be much longer, 'compound' words. Longer words need not worry you. If you look at them carefully you can sometimes spot what they mean from the word parts which have been used. Often, parts of foreign words make up part of a larger word. The more familiar you become with words the more fun you can have with them and the easier they are to understand.

catastrophe

business

Exercise 1

Each of the words below contains a smaller word (a creature) within it. It could be as small as an insect or as large as a whale. See if you can find them.

literature – rat   initial   manufacture   pigment   rather   dogma   share   swiftly   growl   elephant   catalogue

Exercise 2

The words below also have one or more smaller words within them. See if you can find these too.

technology – no, log   handkerchief   disgust   wolfish   slippery   trowel   flour   definitely intelligent   awkward   hospital   shepherd

Exercise 3

Make a list of at least 20 words which contain other words. Use a dictionary to help you.

Spelling strategies

Many people say either that they cannot spell or that they find spelling difficult. When you look carefully at the English language, that is not really surprising. While there are some rules, and spelling patterns we can follow, most of these rules and patterns are broken at some time. However, if we think in terms of words and vocabulary (not of spelling) and expect to be fascinated rather than frustrated, this positive approach will make the task easier.

Think about the ways in which you can learn about words from the text you see every day. This is far more enjoyable than simply memorising a list by heart. Look at the words around you.

• on television   • on buses and trains
• on printed advertisements and packaging
• in books at home and at school…

Here are some ideas which will help you when you do have to learn spellings. But use these methods in advance – not just the night before the test!

Look, cover, write, check   Look at each word in your list for a few seconds, then write it down. Check it against the correct spelling.

Split words between syllables   By splitting words and tapping out each 'beat' you may remember the word. For example, saying *shep-herd* may stop you writing *shepard* in the test.

Use a mnemonic   These are sentences or phrases made from the letters to help you remember something. For example, *Big Elephants Can Always Understand Small Elephants* will help you to spell the word 'because'.

Exercise 1

Use a mixture of strategies to learn ten spellings from the essential spellings list on pages 10 and 11. You can choose any of the subjects, but it might be a good idea to pick one in which you find some of the vocabulary quite difficult.

Exercise 2

Collect 10–12 words (from any subject) that you have met in school during the past couple of weeks. List them in alphabetical order and write the meaning of each word next to it to make a mini glossary. Learn the spelling of the words.

Use what you already know   Some words are compound words, made up of smaller parts. Building on your knowledge may help you, for example *know-ledge, mis-chief, re-member*.

Say what you see   Words do not always sound the way they look. It may help if you say words aloud as they appear on the page phonetically. For example, you might say *silenkee* for *silence* and *sold-eye-er* for *soldier*.

Get help   Ask your friends or family to test you.

Deconstruct and reconstruct   Write out your spelling list, leaving out the vowels (*a, e, i, o, u*). Later, or the next day, try to fill in the correct vowels.

Have some fun   If a word has a **rhythm** or pattern, sing it or make up a rhyme about it, for example, for February try: *Eff Eee Bee Ar You Ay Ar Why, You can't spell it even if you try*.

Active revision   Do something! Just looking at your list is unlikely to help you, but if you do something with the words you may remember them. Draw a sketch or poster to put up in your bedroom. Write a list to put up over your bed or in the bathroom.

Look for patterns   Watch out for the way both consonants and vowels are arranged – there is often no logic to it, but it can help you to remember the spelling. If a word has a double letter or letters write them in a different pen or as capitals, for example *aCCoMModation, poSSeSSion, questioNNaire*. Vowel patterns are also interesting. Notice combinations such as *ie, ei, ai, ia, ou, ous, uous, ue, io*. Think of long vowel combinations as in *beautiful*.

Remember the rules   Spelling rules are not always very helpful and can be confusing. For example, I *before* E *except after* C is no help with words like *weight* and *height*. See spelling rules as general guidelines that are often broken rather than an inflexible instruction.

Exercise 3

Find two or three words which you always have difficulty with. Design a large and colourful poster to help you remember them.

Exercise 4

Choose two or three words (you could use those from Exercise 3 again) and make up a rhyme or mnemonic to help you remember them.

T RED ALERT RED ALERT RED ALERT RED

Essential spellings

- It is important that you can spell accurately in all your school subjects – not just in your English lessons.

- The words below are taken from a variety of subjects and include those which might cause you problems, but most will be familiar to you.

- Use a range of spelling strategies to learn and remember them.

English

advertisement   alliteration   atmosphere
comparison   conjunction   consonant
dialogue   expression   genre   grammar
metaphor   myth   narrator   pamphlet
playwright   preposition   rhyme   rhythm
simile   synonym   vocabulary

Maths

addition   angle   approximately   average   axis   calculate
circumference   co-ordinate   decimal   diameter   division
equilateral   horizontal   isosceles   multiplication   parallel
perimeter   quadrilateral   symmetry   weight

Science

absorb   alkaline   amphibian   apparatus   circulation
condensation   cycle   digestion   dispersal   dissolve
distillation   evaporation   frequency   friction   function
laboratory   liquid   nutrient   oxygen   particles   respiration
solution   temperature   thermometer   vertebrate

History

agricultural   cathedral   chronological   civilisation   constitution
contradiction   disease   dynasty   economy   emigration
government   immigration   independence   parliament   political
priest   propaganda   reign   religious   source

Geography

amenity   contour   country   county   desert   erosion
estuary   function   international   latitude   location   longitude
national   physical   pollution   regional   settlement   situation
transportation   weather

RE

baptism   Buddhism   celebrate   ceremony   Christian
creation   disciple   Hinduism   hymn   immoral   Islam
Judaism   marriage   miracle   Muslim   parable   prejudice
prophet   Sikh   special   spiritual   symbol   synagogue

Music

chord   composition
crotchet   harmony
instrumental   interval
lyric   melody   musician
octave   orchestral
percussion   pitch   quaver
rhythm   semibreve
synchronise   tempo
timbre   vocal

Drama

applause   character   costume   director   dramatise   entrance
exit   improvise   lighting   performance   rehearse   rehearsal
role   scene   script   theatre

Using a dictionary

- A good dictionary is essential, and being able to use one easily and confidently is just as important.

- Try to become familiar with the dictionaries used at school and keep a dictionary at home to help you correct your spellings in all your school subjects.

- Dictionaries are arranged in alphabetical order. This is the most obvious point to most people, but it is surprising how many find it difficult to run through the alphabet aloud or in their head so that they can find a word. Try saying the alphabet as fast as you can – it is possible to say it in about three seconds!

- Dictionaries give useful information. As well as providing the correct spellings of words, dictionaries also give the meaning or meanings, the part of speech and possibly the word root from which the word comes.

- Words that sound the same but have different spellings and meanings are called homophones, for example, *course – coarse*, *sites – sights*, *hair – hare*. Use your dictionary to find pairs of homophones, then write each word in a sentence of its own.

- Dictionary speed test (you will need a stopwatch and enough dictionaries for the group) – in groups of 4 or 5, take it in turns to find an unusual word and read it to the group. Spell the word out or read it to the group. The first person to find the word gets the point. Take it in turns and play five rounds. The player with the most points wins!

- Remember to use a dictionary whenever you come across a new word – don't just guess the meaning.

Using a thesaurus

- Next to a dictionary, a thesaurus is the most useful reference point for any type of writing. It is arranged in a similar way to a dictionary. However, instead of giving you the meaning of a word, it provides you with either another word with a similar meaning or a word with the opposite meaning.

- If you were to look up the word *wet* you would find a list of similar words, or synonyms, such as *soggy, dripping, saturated, soaking, damp, drenched, moist, watery* … You would also find a list of opposites, or antonyms. These might include words such as *arid, dehydrated, desiccated, drained, parched* …

- Be careful to choose a word which is the same part of speech or your replacement word might be completely meaningless.

- You might not always have a thesaurus handy, but you can make an antonym by adding a prefix to the start of a word, for example *appear – disappear, visible – invisible, reliable – unreliable, social – antisocial.*

- It is also possible to add a suffix to the end of a word to change its part of speech – and therefore the job it does, for example *flexible – flexibility, obstinate – obstinacy, rhythm – rhythmic, sensitive – sensitivity.*

- Use a thesaurus whenever you can to make your writing more interesting.

Common errors

However hard you try, you are bound to make mistakes at times. The errors explained in this section are some of the most common. Technical errors are not spelling mistakes but mistakes that have been made by confusing two or more words which sound the same but have different meanings (homophones). Although you will have met all of these words many times before, you may still be getting them wrong.

The letter I Always check your personal writing to see that you have not used a small letter. This is the first person singular and should be written as a capital. Never write *i*.

to/too/two To is generally used when some movement or action takes place (*to make a cake, to the club*). *Too* means more, very, also or as well. Remember, it also has more letters (*too hot, too fast, too difficult*). *Two* refers to the number 2. Think of the words *twice* or *twins* to jog your memory (*two hours ago, two girls*).

there/their/they're There means 'in that place'. If you remove the first letter you still get a place — here (*there it was, up there*). *Their* means 'belonging to them'. This word shows ownership or possession (*their mountain bikes, their team*). *They're* is a shortened form of *they are*. Check by saying it in full when you use it in a sentence. If it makes sense in its longer form, you have probably got it right (*they're going on holiday* — they are going on holiday).

Exercise 1

Suggest words to fill the gaps.
1 The __(two)__ girls asked if they could come _____ the cinema _____.
2 It was _____ hot _____ go for a walk.
3 Sunita's mum asked her _____ get _____ packets of cereal _____.

Exercise 2

Suggest words to fill the gaps.
1 ___(Their)__ shoes were _____ , where they had left them.
2 Polly and her friend pulled _____ hats over _____ eyes.
3 "I wonder if _____ here yet?" Grandad asked _____ mother.

here/hear Here means 'in this place' (*here it is, over here*). *Hear* contains an *ear* – which should remind you of how you hear (*I can hear you*).

are/our/hour Are is part of the verb 'to be', used in the present tense and plural form (*we are, you are, they are*). *Our* means 'belonging to us' (*our family pets, our school team*). *Hour* always relates to time. It is confused with *our* because it sounds the same but, in this case, the first letter is silent (*we waited nearly an hour, the hour had come when we had to leave*).

Some other common mistakes are:

doesn't This is short for 'does not'. If you are in any doubt about its spelling, write it in full. Be careful not to write *dosen't*.

I'm Another contracted or shortened form. In full, this says *I am*. Again, when in doubt, use the longer version. Never use the full version with an apostrophe (*I'am*).

Exercise 3

Suggest words to fill the gaps.
1 We can __(hear)___ the church bells from _____.
2 _____ are some new CDs you might like to _____.
3 Come over _____ so that we can _____ them better.

Exercise 4

Suggest words to fill the gaps.
1 I like __(our)___ house because there _____ people calling in every _____.
2 What _____ of the day _____ they due to arrive?
3 _____ exam will be over in an _____.

15

Character word bank

You probably have several thousand words stored in your head – so why keep using just a few basic ones? For example, when describing a character, try to use a large and interesting combination of carefully-chosen words to create a lively and accurate picture. Here are some adjectives to get you started, divided into antonyms and synonyms.

ugly	gruesome
chatty	outspoken
coarse	rough
ungainly	clumsy
humourless	dull
slow	vague
thoughtless	unsympathetic
reckless	unreliable
ambitious	demanding
moody	listless
obstructive	unsupportive

Exercise 1

1   Use a thesaurus to find five words that you could use to describe a character from a book you have read or from your own writing.

> lively   enthusiastic   friendly   emotional   energetic

2   Then develop your description. When you are thinking about a character the first thing you will probably comment on is their appearance. This is a good starting point – but remember, people are much more than just their physical features. Imagine the person you are describing or thinking about. What, exactly, makes them different or special? What is striking or unusual about them? How do they move? How do they speak? What do they say?

3   Finally, use carefully-chosen words to describe the thoughts and feelings they might have.

RED ALERT   Make your characters lively and visual by giving them thoughts and feelings.   **ALEF**

attractive	handsome
reserved	shy
controlled	elegant
bright	alert
happy	cheerful
refined	smart
amusing	entertaining
thoughtful	sympathetic
careful	cautious
content	complacent
helpful	supportive

Don't forget that a character is almost certain to display a range of characteristics from both columns.

Exercise 2

I   Imagine a situation where you have to rescue someone from a river unexpectedly. You will need to find words that describe your thoughts and feelings before, during and after the event. Here are the thoughts of a character, before the event, written in the first person:

> The sun was warm on my back as I stood lazily watching the float from my line bob up and down with the flow of the river. A feeling of peace and contentment flowed through my body as I thought of the family gathering which was due to take place the next day. Suddenly the peace and silence were shattered ...

2   Continue to describe the events which follow, whilst concentrating on describing your thoughts and feelings.

3   Try this exercise using other story lines:
   • Imagine that someone is expecting a letter in the post – it could be good or bad news. How would they feel as the postman arrives? As they open the letter? As they read it? After the message of the letter has sunk in?
   • Make a list of words which would describe an actor's thoughts and feelings before, during and after a performance on stage.

New words; old words

Understanding the jargon

Dialect is the language peculiar to a particular district or class.

The English language is spoken by millions of people – the majority of them living many miles away from the United Kingdom! There are places with their own form of English that we would probably be able to recognise as English, but it is rather different from our own form.

The English that we know and use is made up of words, word roots, phrases and expressions from all over the world. The language contains words which are Old French, Old German, Norse, Old English, Middle English, Latin and Greek. The English language has also been in the process of change for hundreds of years. Words we use daily have been brought into the language from France, Germany,

Exercise 1

How many words can you find which begin with these Latin or Greek prefixes?
For example: bio → biology.

| bio-   photo-   psych-   sub-   geo-   terra- |

Use your dictionary to help you.

Exercise 2

Find out where the words below come from. For example: discotheque → French.

| spaghetti   risotto   canoe   kayak   jodhpur   vindaloo
lasagne   kaput   pizza   kindergarten   embargo
cul-de-sac   souvenir   gymkhana   shampoo   barbecue
chilli   tomato   igloo   cotton   syrup   zero   sofa   divan
caravan   curry   juggernaut   bungalow   verandah   bangle
dinghy   yoga   pyjamas   bamboo   kangaroo   casserole |

None of them came from England – but they are still part of the English language.

Scandinavia, India, Africa, the Caribbean, Jamaica, America (North and South), Italy, India …

So that every English-speaking person can understand every other English-speaking person, we have what is called **standard English**. Ways of speaking which are special, or only used in one area, are called non-standard English.

- **Greek and Latin word roots**
  Here are some Latin and Greek words you might recognise: *audio, kilo, ultra*.

- **Dialect words**
  Dialect is shown by the choice of words someone uses, and not by how they pronounce them (their accent). For example, in Hampshire, a wasp is called a *jasper*.

- **Foreign words**
  Many words are 'borrowed' from other languages. For example, the French have borrowed the expression *le week-end*, and the English have borrowed the French word *café*.

- **New words**
  Words can change their meaning over time. The word *wicked* used to mean bad or evil, but now it means brilliant or wonderful!

Exercise 3

New words come into the language every year. Look at these words below. Less than fifteen years ago these words were unheard of – they would have meant nothing to your great-grandparents. Write a definition for each one.

| text message | modem | CD-ROM | telesales | internet |
| disk | play station | yuppie | gazump | commuter | DVD |

Parts of speech

Understanding the jargon

A mnemonic is a phrase or word in which the initial letters help you to remember something else.

It is almost impossible to say anything, in speech or writing, without using some of the parts of speech. Although you may recognise the parts of speech when you see or hear them, it is easy to forget the correct name for each one.

First, you can learn the names by remembering a simple mnemonic:

C A N V I P P A

Each letter of this word corresponds to the first letter of one of the parts of speech.

C Connectives (or conjunctions)   Used to join or connect words, phrases, sentences and paragraphs together. They are link words (*but, and, so*).

A Adjectives   Used to describe a noun. They give more information about a thing (*large, fierce dog*).

N Noun   The name of something. It could be a person, place or thing, or a quality or feeling (*pen, girl, town*).

Exercise 1

Here is a 'phrase generator'.

	Adjective	Noun	Verb	Adverb
the	enormous	mongrel	snarled	menacingly
	huge	hound	growled	threateningly
	powerful	dog	grumbled	ominously
	fearsome	cur	warned	loudly

Use the phrase generator to make some interesting sentences and phrases of your own.

> Example
> We could hear the powerful cur snarling ominously from behind the shed.

20

V   Verb   A doing word or word of action. Sometimes hard to spot because they change in shape so often (*shout, sleep, sing*).

I   Interjection   Think of an *injection* – something being jabbed in sharply – to help you to understand this part of speech. Usually short, sharp words showing emotion (*Oh dear!*).

P   Pronoun   *pro* means 'for' and *noun* means 'name'. Used for, or instead of, a noun to avoid repeating the noun (*Lia went to work. She took her lunch*).

P   Preposition   Notice the word *position* within this word. Usually this word tells you where something is in relation to something else (*under, in, over*).

A   Adverb   As with the adjective, this is 'added' to the verb to give more information. It describes the manner in which the action is done and often ends in *-ly* (*quickly, smoothly*).

Strictly speaking, we could add a further letter to our mnemonic:

A   Article   The definite article *the*, and the indefinite articles *a* and *an*.

Exercise 2

1   Draw a blank version of the phrase generator, with the same four headings.
2   List four words of your own under each column.
3   Use the phrase generator to help you express a single idea in a number of different ways.
4   Try different sentences and ideas.

Sentences

You will already have looked in detail at the smallest unit of language – the word – so you know that words can be built up into sentences, paragraphs and, eventually, a whole text.

It is important to know how sentences work if you are going to be able to use them in an effective way. A sentence usually expresses a thought, a fact or an idea. Sentences are then put together in paragraphs. If a sentence is to do its job, it must fit in a way which helps the meaning of the paragraph. Therefore a *sentence must make sense*.

You can use the letters V S O (verb, subject, object) to check whether a group of words is a complete sentence.

Many sentences contain all three of these parts of speech – but some don't.

> Example
> S   V   O
> Mina threw the ball towards the basket.

Exercise 1

Underline the verbs.
1   They are <u>going</u> for a swim.
2   Vikram sat in the corner.
3   Lewis cried very loudly.

Exercise 2

Underline the subjects.
1   <u>Lindsay</u> fell in the river.
2   Most of the team attended the practice.
3   The teacher picked up her books.

Exercise 3

Underline the objects.
1   The children all gave presents to <u>Sarah</u>.
2   The old man was busy digging the garden.
3   The bright lights gave him a headache.

4   Alice gently combed the dog.
5   The whole family watched the film.
6   Grandma really enjoyed eating the sandwich.

Exercise 4

The groups of words below could be either phrases or sentences. Use the two tests to check them.
1   standing by himself in the doorway (phrase)   2   she washed up afterwards
3   he smiled   4   at long last   5   the milkman had arrived
6   round the back   7   the latest thing 8   he went

Sentences and phrases

A further test you can try is to ask yourself if the sentence makes sense standing on its own. If it does not, then it might be a phrase. Phrases still make sense, but only *in context*.

Most sentences have at least a verb and a subject. Phrases don't often have a verb. The group of words *in the corner* have no verb and no subject, so they make a phrase not a sentence. The phrase makes sense only in context.

> ### Example
>
> If someone asks "Where is the cat?" and the reply is "In the corner" then the phrase makes sense in that context.

Clauses

By now you can probably join simple sentences by using connectives to combine several ideas. For the moment, think of a clause as a sentence within a sentence. As with phrases, sometimes a clause makes sense on its own (an independent clause) and sometimes it relies on the other words in the sentence to help it make sense (a dependent clause).

Exercise 5

Write five sentences about each of the following. Link shorter sentences together.

• A visit to a theme park
• A view from a window
• Things seen on a journey

Exercise 6

Copy the main clauses below and add a second clause to make them more interesting.

1 I came home late.
2 We all went ice-skating.
3 My brother has crashed his motorbike.
4 School finishes early tomorrow.

Tactics

Start sentences with a capital letter.

Check there is a subject, an object and a verb.

Link short sentences together to make complex ones.

Finish sentences with a full stop.

RED ALERT RED ALERT RED ALERT RE

Paragraphs

Prose (fiction and non-fiction) is always written in paragraphs. Sentences are constructed by putting words together in a group to make sense. In the same way, paragraphs are groups of sentences which help to give a fuller picture. They are sometimes called blocks of meaning.

Paragraphs are like doing a jigsaw. You need an opening paragraph (introduction) followed by the main text (several, perhaps many, other paragraphs) and an ending paragraph (conclusion).

Paragraphs act as signposts, showing you where an idea starts and where it finishes. Paragraphs also signal a change in direction – a different subject, a shift in time, a move to another place, or that the writer is thinking about another viewpoint.

It is usual to indent paragraphs or to leave a line between paragraphs. Indenting simply means going in from the margin a set distance every time a new paragraph is started. Here is the beginning of a novel, showing the first paragraph not indented (which is usual) with the next, new paragraph indented.

Exercise 1

Try writing a paragraph for each stage of these 'mini-stories'.
1   A boy goes into a shop. He finds he has no money. He leaves the shop.
2   A girl goes to the swimming baths. She sees someone in trouble. She helps them.
3   A new student arrives at school. You talk to them at break. You talk to them again at the end of the day.

Here is an example to help you with the first one.

> Sharif loved the choice of sweets in the supermarket. He never tired of looking at them and imagining the taste of them in his mind. Even the names on the bright packaging made his mouth water. After several minutes of agony, he chose a large chocolate bar and a packet of the gum which his mum said would leave him toothless before long.
>
> Satisfied with his choice, he headed for the checkout with the fewest customers. Even that one was occupied by a man who seemed to be buying enough food to feed Sharif's family for weeks. When his turn eventually came, he watched his own, meagre purchases glide towards the cashier's till and, thrusting his hand into his pocket for the money, he found – nothing!

Example

Despite his flyaway hair, Viking beard and deafening laughter, Laurence was the most courteous, careful and cautious of bus drivers. He was never grumpy, never reckless, never moody. Never.

But being asked to take the rugby club on tour – that was a different matter. A ski trip – no problem. A factory outing – child's play. But fifteen men on a bus meant war had been declared.

Paragraphs usually follow in sequence. This is so that the reader can see the order of events or follow the line of an argument. Sometimes they are in order of time (chronological order), and sometimes the writer looks to the past (a flashback).

Paragraphs help the reader to see what is coming next. A text without paragraphs is difficult to read and understand. Each paragraph should make a main point or points supported by relevant ideas and evidence.

Exercise 1 continued

He headed for the automatic door, as casually as he could. Inside, he did not feel casual, though. The cashier had been kind – but he could feel the eyes of the other customers on him as he left to fetch the money he could now picture, left on his bedroom table.

Tactics

Every piece of writing should have at least three paragraphs: introduction, content and conclusion to show the reader the direction of your work.

RED ALERT RED ALERT RED ALERT RED

Capital letters

Capital letters are used to show the most important words on a page. Being able to spot them is particularly helpful when skimming or scanning a text for the main points or for words of special significance. There are occasions when a capital letter should always be used:

- at the start of a sentence   Never begin a sentence without a capital letter.

- for the letter *I*   As well as being a single letter, this is also a complete word. It is never written as a small letter, even in the middle of a sentence.

- for titles given to people   If there is a title before a name, that should have a capital too: for example: Mr Baxter, Doctor Shah, Reverend Pike.

- for the names of people   All proper names should be written with an initial capital, for example: *Harry, Meena, Smith.*

- for place names   Cities, towns and villages, planets and continents all need a capital letter. Every word in your address should start with a capital letter, for example: *Truro, Asia, Goldfield Close.*

- for brand names   for example: *Adidas, Nike, Kelloggs, Sony.*

- for the titles of books, records, groups   Again, where these are of special importance they should be written in capitals.

- for special words   If a name is particularly important – perhaps having religious significance – it should be given a capital. Many of these are names.

Exercise 1

Copy this piece of writing, adding capital letters where necessary.

> mrs carter shouted upstairs to her two children, ben and kate. it was tuesday morning and they had to be in birmingham to meet the train from london.
>
> "i just want to hear the end of this beatles' song," kate yelled back. ben grabbed his new nike jacket from the landing before racing downstairs.

Nouns

Nouns were probably the first words you ever used as they are simply names for people, objects or things. There are several types of noun which can be a little confusing. But once you have looked at the different types, you will see they are straightforward to learn. You might even know some of them already.

Common nouns   These refer to the name by which something is most often called. Common nouns are used when talking in a general way about an object.

Proper nouns   You would not want to be called just *boy* or *girl*. You have a proper name which is used when people speak to you. Proper nouns are special names – they are much more exact than common nouns. They always start with a capital letter: *Anna, Jacob, Africa*.

Concrete nouns   All nouns are either concrete or abstract. A concrete noun is used for a real, solid object. It does not mean that something is literally made from concrete! For example: *chair, table, sheep*.

Collective nouns
The word for a group or collection of things is called a collective noun: *a flock of sheep*.

Abstract nouns
These nouns are things like feelings, qualities or emotions. They are real enough but you could not touch them, hold them or buy them in a shop. For example: *wisdom, fear, hate, kindness*.

Exercise 1

Here are some collective nouns. What would be in each group?
a pack of (cards)   a bunch of ....   a flock of ....   a herd of ....   a crowd of ....

Exercise 2

What are the collective nouns for these groups of things?

a s(chool) of fish
a l................ of puppies
a t................ of monkeys
a s................ of bears
a m................ of crows

27

Verbs

Verbs (words of action, or doing/being words) can be difficult to spot. Here are some terms which will help you.

Infinitive You could think of this as the name of the verb, or verb family. (If you put the word *to* before a word, it will often show you whether that word is a verb or verb part.)

Examples

to go   to be   to have   to swim
to shout   to need   to forget   to eat

Tense Verbs change according to the time the action takes place. There are three main tenses:

• Past tense: used when you are writing or speaking about yesterday, last week or last year – anything which happened before this moment now (*went, was, had* …).

• Present tense: this tells you what is happening now (*talking, sitting, doing*).

• Future tense: this tells you what is going to happen tomorrow, next week or next year (*am going to, will sit*).

Person Actions need to be linked to someone or something if they are going to make sense. When people are doing the action, whether it is just one (singular) or more than one (plural), we talk about the first, second or third person.

Examples

	Singular	Plural
First person	I	we
Second person	you	you
Third person	she/he/it	they

Exercise 1

Change the verb in these sentences to create a stronger picture for your reader. Each sentence has some suggestions to help you, but try to use your own ideas.

1   We were *frightened* camping in the field on our own.   (petrified, terrified, worried)
    We were petrified camping in the field on our own.

2   Mohammed *sat* in the chair.   (relaxed, sprawled, slumped)

3   The old lady *drank* her coffee.   (sipped, slurped, guzzled)

4   The two cars *bumped* into the wall.   (collided, piled, thudded)

5   Sarah *shouted* the news.   (bellowed, broadcast, yelled)

RED ALERT Use a variety of verbs and adverbs to make your writing **ALE** more interesting.

Agreement Verbs have tense and person and both parts must make sense together – this is called agreement.

> **Examples**
>
> They was late for school again. x
> They were late for school again. ✓

Using verbs It is especially important to select the right verb – they can be very powerful. In your writing try to use verbs and some adverbs, to give your reader a clear and precise picture.

> **Example**
>
> *The walker went through the wood* could be made more interesting by writing *The walker strode/marched confidently/ eagerly through the wood.*

Exercise 2

Write a fantasy story about what happened to you on your holidays. Try to use as many exciting and descriptive verbs as possible.

Then write what you hope will happen on your next holiday. You might continue your adventures from the previous trip, or try something completely new!

RED ALERT RED ALERT RED ALERT RED AL

Punctuation

It would be difficult to drive a car safely if there were no signposts, signals or road markings. In the same way, punctuation marks show a reader when to speed up, when to slow down or stop and when to change gear. It is hard to read writing without punctuation.

Although you will almost certainly know the main forms of punctuation, you should always check your work to see if you can use others to help your reader. Look at the checklist to make sure that you know what the marks show.

(.) full stop
Used at the end of a sentence and to show an abbreviation (shortened form) of a word or words.

> **Example**
>
> Rev. – Reverend   etc. – et cetera

> **Example**
>
> Pens, pencils, rulers and rubbers ...

(,) comma
Used to indicate a shorter pause than a full stop. Often helpful where words are in a list or where a sentence is broken by other words and phrases being added to it.

(;) semi-colon
Used when you could write two separate but closely related sentences. Also used where there is a great deal of information about each item in a list.

> **Example**
>
> His pockets contained an old knife with a broken handle; a old and blunted stub of pencil; several coins ...

Exercise 1

Punctuate these sentences, using the hints to help you.

1   his lunch consisted of an apple chocolate biscuit and three cheese sandwiches
     His lunch consisted of an apple, chocolate biscuit and three cheese sandwiches.
2   run quickly shouted seema the tide is coming in
     (Look at the speech and exclamation sections above.)
3   sadly the injured blackbird died from its injuries
     (There is a slight break in this sentence. Does it need any punctuation?)
4   stay where you are bellowed the firefighter
     (Look in the sentence for clues about the tone of voice.)
5   gemma ive found your trainers they were under your bed all the time
     (There is more than one way to punctuate this. You may want to make it into two sentences.)

(:) colon
Used to balance two equal statements or phrases, and to introduce a list.

> **Examples**
>
> Speak up: speak out.
> You will need: a large pan, three eggs, salt ...

(!) exclamation mark
Used when someone shouts or cries out, in surprise, anger or pain.

(?) question mark
Used to show the end of a question.

(" ") inverted commas
Used to show the exact words of a speaker.

> **Example**
>
> Help! Stop!

> **Example**
>
> "What are you doing?" she asked.

There are other punctuation marks you can use, such as dashes, hyphens and brackets, but a good understanding of the seven marks listed above covers most purposes.

Exercise 2

Write a short story based on any subject you wish. Try to use all the punctuation symbols referred to on these pages – but make sure you use them correctly.

Don't forget to read through and check your writing when you have finished to make sure you haven't made any mistakes.

Connectives

Good writers and speakers make their meaning clear by helping their readers and listeners to follow the order of what they are saying by linking one idea to the next. In a sentence they use connectives (sometimes called conjunctions) to join things together, just as you might in making a list.

Sometimes, rather than write short, repetitive sentences you might link them together to make your writing more effective. It must still make sense, however.

Examples

Hannah took her books, pencil case and folder out of her bag.

Examples

Robert climbed the tree with caution. He still fell and broke his leg.
Robert climbed the tree with caution but he still fell and broke his leg.

Exercise 1

Try to use some connectives to link these sentences.

1 Chloe put the picture on the wall <u>while</u> Thomas cooked the dinner.
2 She fell flat on her face _____ the first performance.
3 Sanjay had _____ walked the dog, after finishing his book.

Exercise 2

Underline the connecting words or phrases in these sentences.

1 Many minerals could be mined in Antarctica, <u>on the other hand</u> this could be an environmental disaster.
2 Jim had never been to Africa before although he had read a lot of books about it.
3 It had been a long cold winter causing the pipes to freeze up.
4 The children laughed loudly at the clown, eventually clapping their hands with joy.

Tactics

Use connectives to link one idea to the next.

Join short sentences together with connectives to make more complex ones.

RED Use key words and connectives very carefully and only if you understand their meaning. ED ALERT RED

Apostrophes

The apostrophe is used for only two purposes:

• contraction

When writing, or speaking, there are some words which we naturally shorten or do not write in full. When you see an apostrophe it is likely that a letter, letters or even a whole word has/have been left out.

Example

Contraction
is not – isn't   does not – doesn't

• to show possession (ownership)

There is a simple trick to test whether you have put the apostrophe in the right place. Draw an imaginary, vertical line where the apostrophe is written. Anything to the left of the line owns what is on the right of it.

Example

Possession
the tools of the plumber – the plumber's tools

Exercise 1

Shorten these words by using an apostrophe.
has not – hasn't   could not   I will   she had   did not

Exercise 2

Try these on your own. Put the apostrophe in the right place.

1   the boys trainers (singular boy) – the boy's trainers
2   the captains decisions (singular captain)
3   the teams results (singular team)
4   a days work (singular day)
5   all the dogs tails (plural dogs)

Tactics

Apostrophes show a letter or letters is/are missing.

Apostrophes show who owns something.

33

Preparing for English work in Year 7

- Many of the topics covered so far will have been familiar. At primary school you will have been asked to learn spellings and completed word work and sentence construction. You will certainly have completed a whole range of writing tasks and had regular opportunities for private reading. The work you will do at secondary school is not so very different.

- What *is* different, and may take a bit of getting used to, is the fact that you are not in the same room all the time. You will also have different teachers for each subject. Whereas you used to have a literacy session every day, now you may have English less often. But don't worry — here is a list of possible differences to help prepare you for secondary school.

- Equipment   Because you need to move around the school, you need to carry your equipment with you. Check that you have pens, pencils, ruler, rubber, felt-tipped pens, crayons and so on to take to every lesson. (A small dictionary will be helpful in all your subjects.) Keep larger items at home, for example reference books.

You will obviously have a school bag, but a hard-back file is useful just to keep work flat and clean. Even in your bag, loose papers will get crumpled and worn on your journey to school. Transparent zip files are also useful; they can be used to carry work to school and (if they have a clear name label) can be handed in and returned for use time and time again. But do not use single, plastic envelopes for each individual sheet of paper in a story or project — each one has to be removed for marking, which makes life difficult for your teacher!

- **Reading**   The reading you do at secondary school will be similar to that at your primary school — just a bit more advanced. You will still read, but you may be asked to read on your own more often.

- **Writing**   You need to remember everything that you were taught at primary school. You will be asked to write for many different purposes — most of them are explained in the next section of this book. You also need to present your work carefully (see the presentation guidelines below).

- **Presentation**   Most of your work will be handwritten, but you could word-process it — at home or at school. However, remember that your work will be marked on how good it is, not on how pretty it looks. Some things are better written by hand and for others the computer could be more appropriate. Here is a checklist to help you assess your presentation.

  - Does the work fit the purpose? Does it interest, amuse or entertain ? Is it informative, thoughtful and convincing?

  - Does the work suit its audience? Is it meant for a special group, for others your own age, for your teacher or for a general audience?

  - Is it neat and clear?

  - Have you used sentences and paragraphs if it is a story or essay, or lines if it is a poem?

  - Check your vocabulary, punctuation and grammar.

  - If you needed pictures, maps, headings, diagrams, borders, colour or different font styles, did you include them? Be careful not to overdo it!

  - Are you proud of your work?

If you have answered 'yes' to all of these questions, congratulations!

Organising your homework

You will almost certainly have been set homework tasks at primary school, so the process will be familiar to you. In Year 7, however, you are likely to get much more and in a greater number of subjects. Few schools make homework optional — so it cannot be avoided! Homework is designed to help you, not just keep you busy. It follows up and supports work learned in class to make sure that you have understood and remembered important topics and to prepare you to move on to the next stage with confidence. The following are some ideas to help you cope with homework.

- **Listen** Instructions about homework are usually made very clear. Often, the homework task will be linked to a topic which you have been working on during the course of the week and you may have been working on it for some time. You may be asked to write up a final draft of a story, learn for a test or do some research to help you in a future lesson. Listen carefully to the key words your teacher uses: Redraft... , Complete... , Learn... , Find out about... , Make notes... , Read to the end of... , Practise... , Prepare an account of...

- **Write it down** Don't think "I'll remember that" — you won't! At secondary school you are too busy to remember everything you are asked to do in a typical day. Write the details of the homework task clearly and briefly in your homework notebook or school diary. Make sure that you record the subject, the day the work was set, what the task involves and when it must be given in. You will probably not have enough space to write too much, so keep it simple. If more information is available (perhaps on a worksheet or in a textbook) then refer to it in your diary.

Date set	Subject	Date due
Mon 12/4	English: complete first draft of story	19/4
	Science (no H/W set)	
	(Youth Club: 7.30)	
Tue 13/4	French: See vocab list	20/4
	REMEMBER outdoor kit for P.E. next week.	20/4
	Play rehearsal 4.00 - 5.00	
Wed 14/4	Maths: Ex 3 + 4 p120	16/4
	Science - Topic research	19/4

- **Organise your time** As well as having a school timetable, you should also have a personal timetable. You will need to plan carefully to allow for other activities such as clubs, practices, rehearsals and free time. Check your homework book regularly and not just in the morning. Look ahead — at this week and next.

- **Organise your equipment** Do you have everything you need to do the task? You may need a variety of resources, such as exercise books and textbooks, paper and reference materials. Will you need to go to the library or use a computer?

- **Ask for help** Your teacher will prefer to deal with any problems you might have in doing your homework earlier rather than later. Speak to him or her before you take the homework home if you do not understand what you have been asked to do. If you find you have problems when you get home, then speak to your teacher before the lesson (not during) when the work needs to  be handed in. Don't make excuses — they have all been tried at some time! Take in a note from home if you have a genuine reason for not completing work. Above all, be honest and then your teacher can help you clear up any confusion.

- **Remember to bring it back to school** Doing your homework is very important, but your assignment cannot be marked if it is left in your bedroom or on the kitchen table. So put your homework in your school bag the night before so that you can take it in and give it in.

- **Remember** Listen; write the homework down in your diary; organise your time; check your diary; ask for help if you need it; take your homework in and hand it in on time.

Fiction texts and book reviews

Understanding the jargon

To review literally means 'to look at again'. A book review describes your thoughts and feelings about a book.

At primary school you will have looked at books, stories and extracts and been expected to comment on them. You may have designed a cover for a book you have, or have written the 'blurb' to go on the back. At secondary school you will probably be asked to develop this and write a simple review.

In the same way that you look at a text (fiction or non-fiction) in class and discuss it, writing a review involves going through the same process. The difficulty is that at secondary school you will be expected to work on your own at some stage. You will be given a good deal of help and guidance, but you should now be able to work independently.

Here is a checklist to use to help you. You will not be expected to write a very complicated review in Year 7, but you should consider as many of the following ideas as possible. (You might not be able to answer every question for every book, but use them to help you think.)

- Background What made you choose the book? When and where is it set? In the past, present or future? In this country or another? In what sort of area?

- Genre What type of book is it? Mystery, fantasy or adventure …?

Exercise 1

Look again at a book you have just read, or are reading at the moment. Think about the book in terms of the guidelines above. Write down, in note form, the main important points referring to your book. Try this with other types of books, such as non-fiction, poetry and plays.

Exercise 2

Try this same formula with a video you have watched.

RED ALERT Don't just rewrite the story when reviewing a book – ALE
give your views too.

- Summary What was the book about? How would you tell the story to a friend, as briefly as possible? (Do not just rewrite the story for your review!) Were there any subplots?

- Characters Comment on the main characters. How well did the author describe them? Were they believable? Who were your favourite and least favourite characters? Was there a character with whom you sympathised? Was the story told from one character's point of view?

- Language Think about the word choices the author has made. What kind of tone has he or she created? Why? Does it suit the style of the book? Is the language of the book easy or complex? How well are scenes described?

- Themes, messages and morals Was there anything in the book which was supposed to make the reader think, or pose questions? Did you have to look at a particular subject from a new angle? Was there a moral to the story? Did the story explore themes or examine problems?

- Criticism Summarise your enjoyment of the book. Which were the best and the worst parts? Remember that criticism does not mean that you look only at the negative points – try to be positive as well. Support your points with quotations from the book.

- Recommendation Would you recommend the book to a friend? Who would it suit? Have you read any other books by the same author? How does this book compare? If you met the author, what questions would you ask them? What comments would you make to them about the book?

Exercise 3

Use the notes you have made in the previous exercises to design a book and video jacket. Consider how the jacket and box might look. Who is the audience? What age groups are they? How might you appeal best to those readers/viewers? How can you make the book or video sound appealing? What reviews might you include on the back?

Tactics

Be honest in your book review but make sure that you give evidence and examples to support what you say. Use the guideline headings to help you.

RED ALERT RED ALERT RED ALERT R

Genre

Genre (pronounced 'john-rah') simply means types of writing. Once an author has decided whether to write fiction or non-fiction, they must choose a genre in which to write. Here are a few examples.

Fiction

Thriller / Adventure
Romance
Science fiction
Ghost story
Crime / Mystery

Exercise 1

Read these extracts. What genre do they belong to?

1   *Tharg tranced into the intergalactic   transformer just in time. As he left the mother ship he could see its force shield shake with the power of the latest onslaught. His detector display revealed that they were gathering for a fresh attack – he changed course to avoid it...*

2   *The moon glinted coldly on the gravestones in the church yard. The yew trees dripped wet with the night rain and owls hooted. Muted sounds echoed off the walls and settled dully in the shadows...*

3   *The arch of Abigail's neck and the flecks of her hair were silhouetted against the ballroom window by the light of the October moon. Simon stepped lightly through the french windows and clasped her firmly...*

Non fiction

Autobiography / Biography
Travel writing
Diary
Humour
Report
Manual

Elements from different genres can be combined – a diary may contain humour, a thriller may have a romantic element – but there is usually one main genre. It is possible to spot the genre of a piece of writing by looking at the writer's choice of words – the way the sentences are put together and the tone, pace and atmosphere.

Exercise 1 continued

Extract 1 is from the genre of science fiction. You could probably tell by the use of words such as *intergalactic* and *force shield*. The writer's choice of the name *Tharg* will have told you that the story was not about everyday life. The sentences are quite short and there is a sense of movement. In contrast, extract 3 uses words, names and verbs that are much calmer and softer.

Look again at extract 2. Try writing your own opening paragraph using the same subject matter and ideas.

Exercise 2

Now try a first paragraph for a piece from another genre. Look again at the list of types to help you.

Looking at poetry

It is difficult to say exactly what poetry is – it would be easier to say what it is not! For this reason many students find poetry a tricky subject.

The difficulty arises because poetry takes many forms. It can be a short rhyming poem; a longer poem telling a story (in ballad form); a free verse poem without rhyme or a descriptive poem. Whatever the poem, it is written in lines and verses (sometimes called stanzas) whereas prose is written in sentences and paragraphs.

When you are writing an account of an event or a story using prose, you can give a lot of detail. A poem is not usually as long as a piece of prose and there is little opportunity for piles of information. The aim is to give your reader a snapshot of the things you see, think or feel. You need to choose your words very carefully – each one has a job to do. Read the poem on page 43 by Jenny Joseph, then think about the points below.

- **Form** This poem does not have a definite or regular shape. It has four stanzas with a different number of lines in each one. It has no rhythm or rhyme.

- **Words** The words in the poem have been chosen with care. There are probably very few which you have not heard before, but together they conjure up a picture. Think about why the colour purple was chosen. Why are words like *gobble*, *sausages*, *spit* and *satin sandals* used?

- **Lines** Each line of the poem is like a separate picture. You can imagine every part as a little scene. In the same way that the words all help the meaning along, so the lines all build up the impression you are left with at the end.

- **Voice** The 'voice' of a poem means the person or thing speaking. In this case Jenny Joseph is speaking about her own feelings and views. But notice that although she starts with the first person singular (*I*) she also says *you* and *we* as well. Why do you think she does this?

Exercise 1

Now write your own poem. Choose a bird or animal to write about. Make your poem between six to twelve lines long, and it doesn't have to rhyme. Use the name of the creature only in the title; do not mention it anywhere else. Keep the title a secret and see if a friend can guess what the creature is from your poem.

• Message Once you have read the whole poem you are left with some images, or pictures, in your mind, but what is the main point of the whole poem? It could be summarised by saying 'When I get old I will behave eccentrically instead of sensibly as I have to now.'

Warning

When I am an old woman I shall wear purple
With a red hat that doesn't go, and doesn't suit me,
And I shall spend my pension on brandy and summer gloves
And satin sandals, and say we've no money for butter.
I shall sit down on the pavement when I'm tired
and gobble up samples in shops and press alarm bells
And run my stick along the public railings
and make up for the sobriety of my youth.
I shall go out in my slippers in the rain
And pick the flowers in people's gardens
And learn to spit.

You can wear terrible shirts and grow more fat
And eat three pounds of sausages at a go
Or only bread and pickle for a week
And hoard pens and pencils and beermats and things in boxes.

But now we must have clothes that keep us dry
And pay our rent and not swear in the street
And set a good example for the children.
We must have friends to dinner and read the papers.
But maybe I ought to practise a little now?
So people who know me are not too shocked and surprised
When suddenly I am old, and start to wear purple.

Exercise 2

Now write a short poem about another animal or bird. This time, refer to your creature as 'he' or 'she' and use words that make the reader think of the creature in human terms (personification). Don't mention your animal or bird in the poem, but try to make the reader picture the creature through the scene. Here is an example for you.

The Eagle
He clasps the crag with crooked hands;
Close to the sun in lonely lands,
Ring'd with the azure world, he stands.

The wrinkled sea beneath him crawls;
He watches from his mountain walls,
And like a thunderbolt he falls.

Alfred, Lord Tennyson

Tactics

Think about the form you are using.

Choose your words carefully.

Don't use a word just to make it rhyme.

43

Projects and topics

Sources and resources

- **Projects and topics are set at school to improve your knowledge of a subject and to test your ability to find things out by doing some research.**

- **The difficult part is in finding something to say — the easy part is that there are many places to look.**

TOPIC

The written word books: encyclopedias, specialist books, media: magazines, newspapers, libraries: school, town

Technology computer, CD-ROM, internet, email addresses, websites

Places museums and exhibitions, tourist information, noticeboard, Post Office, police station, specialist shops

The past county archives, local history society, local paper records

People teachers, family and friends, specialist groups, local and national groups, clubs and fan clubs

Sight and sound television programmes, films, radio, music, audio and videotapes, CDs, DVDs, media

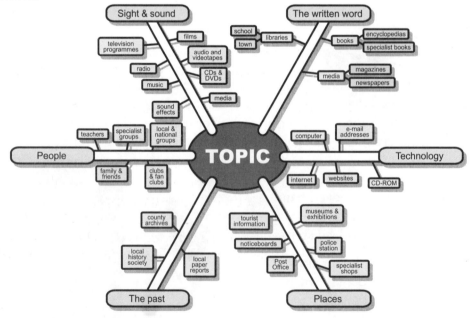

- There are many routes you could take to find what you want. It is very important that you make notes as you go. Only use reliable and up-to-date sources. Always write down where you got any information from and put that in your project in the bibliography, references or sources section.

Writing it up

- Once you have done the research on your project, look back at the instructions for the task. Does your research match the type of work you are expected to do? Have you collected too much information or wandered off the main subject?

- Before putting your project together you need to decide very carefully which area, or areas, of the subject you are going to write about. You may need to narrow down to a part of a subject. For example, instead of writing about sport, you might focus on one sport.

- If you have done your research properly you will have plenty to say – but don't try to say everything! Be prepared to leave some things out, if necessary – it is important to select your material with thought. Use the list below to help you:

Cover and title page

Contents list	number the pages
Introduction	say, briefly, what the project is about
Main content	divided into chapters or sections, with clear headings
Conclusion	summarise your ideas and thoughts
Sources	make a list, saying where you got your information

Optional extras:

Illustration	sketches, diagrams, maps, photographs
Index	with page numbers
Glossary	explanations of unusual words
Appendix	any extra information (diagrams, forms, tables)
Acknowledgements	the names of any organisations that helped you
Dedication	mention someone as a sign of respect or affection

Looking at non-fiction

Non-fiction texts contain facts, as opposed to fiction texts which are imaginary stories and poems. Accounts of things which happened – articles, reports, instructions, reference books, guide books and manuals – are all non-fiction.

The following guidelines will help you to write an article. They could also be used to help you at other times when you are writing news items.

- Headlines and subheadings Make sure you invent an eye-catching headline which summarises the whole story if possible. Use subheadings to signal what is coming next.

- First paragraph Use bold print for the first paragraph. Summarise the main point of your article in this paragraph.

- Tone and style The tone of your article should fit the content, for example a great success for the school team would not be written about in the same tone as a miserable defeat. The tone of many pieces of non-fiction writing is impersonal – the writer is not involved, only giving the facts. You may, however, give opinions – your own and those of other people.

- Reporting and interviewing Report the facts as accurately as you can. Summarise what people say (indirect/reported speech), or use their own words (direct speech), being careful to put their spoken words in inverted commas, as a quotation.

Exercise 1

Complete this task.

Task:	*to write an article for a school magazine or newsletter (150 words)*
Subject:	*report on a school event or function, for example drama performance, sports event, trip or club*
Purpose:	*to interest, inform and entertain*
Audience:	*students (11–16) but also their parents*
Research:	*Interview staff and students. Examine newspapers for ideas on layout, reporting and interview skills.*

RED ALERT Presentation, style and content are all important when **ALE** producing a piece of non-fiction.

Look at the notes Sharon has written for her school newspaper.

Headline:
placard: 'Fare's Fair!'

Notes:
* demonstrators at the bus station
* East Berkham
* local residents angry
* proposed bus fare increase
* up 10%
* expensive for daily commuters
* council say prices too low for too long

They will help her to organise her article logically.

• Layout Decide how to present your work – in columns (some software will help you here) or as a straightforward article.

• Paragraphs Check that the paragraphs follow in the correct order, that one leads naturally to the next, and that you have a clear conclusion.

Exercise 2

Now try this activity.

Task: to design an advertisement (on one side of an A4 sheet)
Subject: a computer with a new style and design
Purpose: to inform and persuade
Audience: adults with school-age children
Research : Question adults and children. Examine advertisements of all types.

Things to think about here include:
• The name Think of a catchy name, motto or jingle which will help sell the computer.
• Appeal What has the computer got which is special or different? What 'extras' does it offer? Is it cheaper, better, more reliable or more versatile than the rest?
• Impact Use colour, different fonts or writing styles, pictures, diagrams and illustration to attract your customers.

47

The writer's workshop

Getting started with stories

Writing a good story is a very difficult business. Good writing of any sort takes a lot of thought and planning. No one can be expected to write brilliantly at a moment's notice. Even when a piece of writing is completed, a writer will alter and redraft it – perhaps many times.

You might find it quite daunting to be asked to write a story. That's understandable as there are many things to consider – What should the story be about? How will it begin and end? Where are you going to get your ideas from?

In park
Saw old man walking two very lively Yorkshire terriers. He wore a cap pulled down over his eyes and was hunched up in his light brown jacket. Looked lonely.

Old lady at garden centre. Keep off grass - She walked all over it. Signs saying 'Do not touch' - She handled all the plants. Then I saw her bump into the fruit tree display. Eye problem?

Story idea - Old man and lady as a couple. Past history? Where do they live?

Writers and authors face the same problems. They get their ideas from exactly the same place you do! They use their own experiences and imagination. They are thoughtful and observant, they notice things around them and jot down their ideas and feelings so that they can use them later.

Roald Dahl kept his story ideas in an old exercise book. He wrote a few sentences when an idea came to him and used them as the basis for a story. Artists often have a sketch book to record things they see and like – you could do the same.

Exercise 1

You may already have an English journal which you use to jot ideas down in. If you don't, try starting a Literacy Log. In it you can note down words you have heard and like; descriptions of people and ideas for stories. You might also stick in pictures or newspaper headlines which appeal to you.

Writer's block

You have probably heard of writer's block. If, after brainstorming ideas for your story and looking through them, you have still not made a start, what can you do? One idea is to ask yourself some questions like those below. (They all contain the letter W which might make them easier to remember.)

- When? Where?   Think about the setting of your story.

- Who?   Decide on the characters you are going to use. Your story might be based on a central character. (Try not to have too many people or it can get complicated.)

- What?   Write down ideas for what might happen in your story. The main storyline is called a plot. Always try to write at least two or three plots – you can then choose the best one or use ideas from each.

- How?   In sorting out your plot, think about how you will begin and end your story.

- Why?   Use this as a general question together with those which you have already asked yourself. Why do your characters behave as they do? Why do events happen in a particular order?

Formula writing

You could use a set order to provide a basic plot. Try an idea like the game 'Consequences': X met Y at ... He said ... She said ... and the consequence was ... . Or you might set a scene: introduce a small number of characters; bring in a problem, crisis, disaster or conflict; show how the problem turns out in the end.

Writing frames

Like formula writing, writing frames are only meant to get you started. You will have seen them before. They usually take a similar approach to the W questions and should only be used to help you in the planning stage. Do not be tempted to just fill in the boxes and leave your story like that. You must expand on and develop your ideas.

Exercise 2

Using the W formula above, note three plot ideas on each of these subjects:
1   Camping disaster
2   The journey
3   The winner!

Example
'Camping disaster'

When?   The wettest May since records began
Where?   The Lake District, near Lake Coniston
Who?   Josie and James, and their dad (single parent)

49

Read on: write on

At secondary school you will meet many different types of writing and, by Year 11, be expected to complete a wide range of reading and writing tasks in a variety of subjects. So it is very important that you have seen as many forms and styles of writing as possible. You will find it difficult to write a ghost story, a report, a newspaper article, an advertisement or a playscript if you have not read or seen one.

It is also just as important that you learn to read more widely for your own enjoyment. You may be a keen reader or you might find reading difficult – it may be that you can never find just the right book for you.

Here are some ideas to help you meet different writing styles and find books to suit you.

- **Ask your friends** Look at what your friends are reading – particularly those with similar interests. A book which is popular with someone else your age may appeal to you as well. Ask them if there is a book or author they would recommend. They may lend you books or swap with you. If so, make sure you all look after each other's books and return them in good condition.

- **Ask your teacher** If you have enjoyed a book or extract which you have read at school, ask your teacher if they know of other books by the same person.

- **Visit the school library** Both school and class libraries have books suitable for your age group. Look in the fiction and non-fiction sections. You are sure to find a story to read and books to help you in your other subjects, as well as books about your hobbies and interests.

Exercise 1

Keep a reading record of the main things you read. Check it to make sure that you do not keep to one author or one subject. Read as widely as possible. Draw up columns in your record book for the date, title of the book, author's name and so on. Give the book a mark out of ten or a star rating.

Date	Subject	Date due
12 Feb	Harry Potter and the Philosopher's Stone (F)	
	Finished. Excellent! ***** (5 stars)	
14 Feb	Fitness For You (NF)	
16 Feb	Learning Badminton (NF)	
20 Feb	Started Watership Down (F)	
	Really good so far.	
2 March	History of Dinosaurs (NF)	
3 March	Handbook of Sport (NF)	

- Join the local library There is certain to be a library in your nearest town or city. If you live in the countryside, there is probably a free mobile library which stops near your house.

- Look at home Older brothers and sisters may be able to think of a book which you would like. Your parents and other relatives will have ideas – they may buy you a special book as a present.

- Look in book shops Book shops stock an enormous choice of fiction and non-fiction, reference books, magazines, newspapers and comics to suit all ages and interests. Don't be afraid to look in second-hand book shops, jumble sales and market stalls.

- Use the internet If you use an internet site to buy books (such as Amazon) look out for recommendations from readers who bought the same books as you.

- Be adventurous Experience of different types of reading will help you to cope with all sorts of written assignments in the future. Even if the texts in the list below would not be your first choice, at least take the time to become familiar with what they are like. Many of them are examples which you might take a brief look at rather than read regularly.

   newspapers: tabloid (small, popular and easy to read, but sometimes over-sensational)
   broadsheet (larger and more serious)
   local papers, magazines (notice the layout, headlines and captions)

   advertisements, posters, technical books, manuals and recipe books, instruction books, text on the television, websites and the internet, reference books, CD-ROMs

Exercise 2

Imagine you are on an alien planet. You can see an extraordinary city stretching out in front of you, and there is a space buggy approaching. Jot down some brief notes about this planet, why you are there and how you feel as you see the buggy get nearer. Now try to write up your notes as a newspaper report, an advertisement, a travel guide and a diary entry.

The writer's toolbox

Understanding the jargon

Alliteration means repeating the consonants.
Assonance means repeating the vowels.
Onomatopoeia is created when the sound of a word echoes its meaning.
Simile suggests one thing is similar to or like another (remember similar).
Metaphor suggests one thing is or has become another (remember metamorphosis).

In any writing task there are many things to think about and a vast number of ways in which the writer can use his or her skill: by using short sentences and limiting the amount of description, the pace of a story can be speeded up; a careful choice of words and names can give exactly the right atmosphere; trouble taken in building up characters makes them lifelike and believable to the reader.

All these literary devices show the skill of the writer – and may take a long time to learn. But there are some 'tricks of the trade' that you know and can use.

• Alliteration and assonance A writer may repeat a word or a phrase, especially if they want to emphasise something important. Alliteration and assonance are ways of emphasising words or sounds so that the reader pays particular attention to them.

Alliteration is simply the repetition of consonant sounds. Hard, jarring consonants can give one effect:
She heard the rasp of the rake and the grind of the gravel...

... while gentler and softer vowels can create a very different picture:
Pollen-laden bumble bees busied themselves in the borders.

Exercise 1

Write five sentences which have an example of alliteration or assonance in them, like the example.

> The clever, cunning, creature crept up quickly.

Exercise 2

Collect ten examples of onomatopoeia, like these:

> splish splash   drip drop

- **Assonance** Assonance is similar to alliteration – but, in this case, the vowel sounds are repeated:
  We sat at ease while the spring breeze lazily swayed the trees.

- **Onomatopoeia** This device also uses sound, but in a different way. Some words sound exactly like the thing they are describing:
  tick tock, clunk click, clip clop.

tick
tock

- **Similes and metaphors** Both of these are examples of what is called imagery as they make the reader use their imagination. Good examples can help the reader to get a vivid picture in their mind.

When you think of similes, think of the word *similar*. Similes are easy to spot as most of them contain the words *as* or *like*.

Be careful when using similes – always try to use unusual and interesting ones. Avoid those you have heard many times before – these are known as clichés. Some well-known ones are:
as blind as a bat, as daft as a brush, as white as snow.

Whereas with similes we say that one thing is *like* another, with metaphors we are saying, in a way, that one thing *has become* something else. Think of the scientific word *metamorphosis* which describes a change – like a caterpillar changing into a butterfly.

> **Example**
>
> Simile: The sky was painted with vivid colours
> Metaphor: The sky was a vivid painting

Exercise 3

Fill in the gaps below to create some similes. Try to make them interesting – don't just write down the first thing you think of.

as black as (the devil's robe)   as tough as...................................
as wrinkled as.............................   as smooth as.................................
as straight as..............................   as sour as....................................
as solid as...................................
as busy as...................................
as sticky as..................................
as strong as.................................
he ran like...................................
she moved like..............................

Tactics

Can I make my writing more interesting?

What skills can I use?

Can I improve the pace and rhythm?

53

Handwriting

By Year 7 you will have already have found a style of handwriting which suits you – but it may not suit other people! If you are not happy with your handwriting, or people find it difficult to read, here are some tips to help you.

- Good handwriting should be clear, readable and cursive (joined up). Any style you choose should be easy to read for you (when you look back at it later), and for anyone else. You may need one style for notes, planning and quick work and another style for neat, finished work. Remember clear, neat writing is required in every subject, not just English.

- Use the right equipment. The ideal type of pen to use is a cartridge or fountain pen. Both can be fitted with different nibs – including nibs for left-handed people. This type of pen helps to create a good style.

- If changing cartridges or filling your pen daily from an ink bottle is a problem, then keep this type of pen for work which you do at home. Instead, take a good quality ballpoint or roller ball pen to school. It does not need to be an expensive one but it must not blot or smudge.

- Use black or blue ink. Keep other coloured inks and pens for special tasks.

- Use lined paper, plain paper with a line guide behind or a ruled handwriting book.

Exercise 1

Try linking the letters in the words below, paying attention to your handwriting style.

1 mad, lad, sad, had, bad, glad, dad, pad

2 play, may, say, clay, day, ray, jay, way, lay

Exercise 2

The following sentence contains all the letters in the alphabet. Copy it, making sure that you link all the letters up correctly.

> The quick brown fox jumps over the lazy dog.

Stop immediately if you get tired or start to make mistakes. ALE

- Make sure you are comfortable. Sit in an upright chair and use a desk or table which is not too high – no higher than the bottom of your breastbone. Keep both feet flat on the ground. Hold the paper or exercise book with your non-writing hand – don't use this hand to support your head.

- Don't grip your pen too tightly. It should be supported by the middle finger of your writing hand and steadied by your thumb and forefinger. If you have difficulty holding a pen properly then use a pen hold, handwriting triangle or elastic bands wound round your pen to get a good grip.

- If you are left handed, use a cushion or a higher chair at home. At school, sit on the left side of a right-handed classmate so that you do not nudge each other.

- Most people have handwriting which is either upright or leans to the right or to the left. Look at your handwriting. Keep to one way – not all three!

- Upper case (capital) letters should be roughly twice the size of lower case (small) letters:

Aa Cc Ee

However, some letters have ascenders (part going up):

Kk Hh Dd

... and some have descenders (a tail hanging down):

Gg Pp Yy

... or both:

Ff

- Don't forget you can change and improve your handwriting at any time.

Exercise 3

Experiment with different pens and use various writing styles to copy out this poem by Edward Lear.

> There was an old man with a beard,
> Who said, "It is just as I feared,
> Two owls and a hen,
> Three larks and a wren,
> Have all built a nest in my beard."

Tactics

Ask your teacher for advice.

Ask your friends and family which styles they find easiest to read or most attractive.

RED ALERT RED ALERT RED ALERT RED ALE

Forms of writing

In English, writing is found in three main forms or shapes:

      prose   **poetry**   **plays**

Plays, when they are written down, are called scripts or playscripts.

Poems are written in lines and verses (or stanzas) which are formed into a variety of forms such as limericks, ballads, haiku, odes, sonnets and so on. Some of these forms have rhythm and rhyme – some do not.

Prose is generally written in sentences and paragraphs which are put together in a way that best fits their purpose and audience. Prose writing can be serious or formal, light-hearted or informal:

Form	Formal	Informal
Essay, exam question, project	✓	
Story, poem, play	✓	
Letter of thanks		✓
Letter of complaint or apology	✓	
Postcard to older relative	semi-formal	
Postcard to close friend		✓
Email to an unknown person or group	✓	
Email to close friend or relative		✓
Advertisement for local or national press	✓	
Advertisement for school magazine	semi-formal	
Shopping list		✓
Diary		✓
Book review	✓	
Report, account, news article	✓	
Instructions, explanations	✓	

Exercise 1

Look back at some of your own formal and informal writing which has been written for different purposes and different people. Does it fit the circumstances it was meant for? Check your writing against the information above.

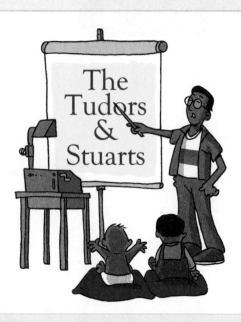

You can see from the table on page 56 that most writing is formal. As a rough guide, if your writing could be printed in a book to be read many years later then it is probably formal. Essays and stories would therefore be in the formal category, but a note, shopping list or memo would not. Letters to friends, email messages and some advertisements might fall somewhere in the middle – we could call these semi-formal.

One of the reasons that most writing is formal is that it needs to be clear, accurate and easy to understand by a wide and varied audience. Unlike situations when you are speaking, you don't have a chance to repeat what you are saying – to confirm that your reader understands you or to explain something in a number of different ways.

With most formal writing tasks, you don't need to get it right first time. Having thought about your purpose and audience you can then draft your work with care, making sure you communicate your thoughts, ideas, demands or instructions without any confusion.

The best way to communicate formally is by writing in standard English. This will be widely understood – even by people you do not know and have not met. The opposite, non-standard English, can be used in writing to a very close friend – there might be words, phrases and expressions which only the pair of you understand, you may use slang or dialect words. To an outsider, this would be like a code which they might have difficulty breaking. For most writing tasks – particularly at school   keep to standard English.

Exercise 2

Visit your school library. Look at the shelves which contain books on all your school subjects (non-fiction). Write down the number of each section. (These are the Dewey system numbers.) Next, look in the fiction section. Are the books arranged in alphabetical order, using the surname of each author?

Dewey numbers

500 – Pure Science	600 – Applied Science
700 – Arts	800 – Literature
900 – History and Geography	920 – Biography

Planning and drafting

Understanding the jargon

Brainstorming means writing down all your ideas about a subject.

Planning

A blank sheet of paper can be quite daunting. No one can be expected to write brilliantly at a moment's notice. Even professional writers need to spend time thinking of ideas and gathering information before they start. You are a writer – so you need to plan like one.

• When you are set a writing task, think about it carefully before you even pick up a pen.

• Then brainstorm your ideas, writing them on a sheet of paper in the form of a list, topic web, spider diagram or mind map.

• Include ideas, feelings, words and sources of help and information in your planning. This is your starting point. You may not need to use all of the information. Just select what is important and, perhaps, add more thoughts and ideas as you go.

58

Drafting

- Before you start drafting your ideas into a piece of text, think about:

  Purpose   What is your writing aiming to do? Inform? Interest? Entertain?
  Audience   Who is going to read it? Adults? Children? Both?

- If there is a clear order to what you are going to write, make a numbered list of the intended content – this will give you a framework for your paragraphs. If there is no clear order, think again.

- Start to write ideas in note form under each section. Cross through anything which seems odd or out of place. Gradually, you will begin to see a complete picture.

- In the example web diagram on page 58, ideas listed under 'Introduction' form paragraphs one and two of the draft shown right. 'Safety' is the basis for paragraph three and the ideas under 'Now' and 'Next' come towards the end of the draft in paragraph nine.

- Remember that this is your first draft. You can still change the paragraph numbers, put other paragraphs in, change the way you say things (expression) and the words you use (vocabulary).

- Make sure that you are happy with the order of your work. Check it carefully for any mistakes in spelling and punctuation before writing up your final draft.

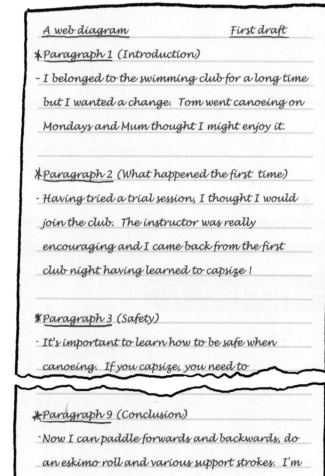

A web diagram   First draft

*Paragraph 1 (Introduction)

- I belonged to the swimming club for a long time but I wanted a change. Tom went canoeing on Mondays and Mum thought I might enjoy it.

*Paragraph 2 (What happened the first time)

- Having tried a trial session, I thought I would join the club. The instructor was really encouraging and I came back from the first club night having learned to capsize !

*Paragraph 3 (Safety)

- It's important to learn how to be safe when canoeing. If you capsize, you need to

*Paragraph 9 (Conclusion)

- Now I can paddle forwards and backwards, do an eskimo roll and various support strokes. I'm good enough to be in the slalom team...

Beginnings and endings

Beginnings

The first word, sentence and paragraph of your writing are what your audience will first read. Of course, you will want to interest them enough to read on. You must start in the best way possible if you are going to grab their attention. You know that you should avoid *Once upon a time ...* and *One day ...*. Here is a poor beginning to a story:

> ### Example
>
> One fine day, Nick walked along the towpath towards Chloe's house. He hoped that he might see her by chance. He had been there before for the same reason ...

There are better ways to begin this story:

- Start from a different point   By striking out *One fine day* the story could begin *Nick walked along the towpath towards ...*

- Use a flashback   Give some information

> ### Example
>
> Nick had seen Chloe from the towpath near her house several times before. He hoped he might see her there today – just by chance.

Exercise 1

1   Read this beginning to a story.

Once upon a time there was an old man walking through London in the pouring rain looking for somewhere to stay.

2   Now rewrite the beginning using some of the other techniques suggested.

> The rain lashed down and the streets of London looked cold and unfriendly as the old man looked wearily for somewhere to stay.

A good beginning and a good ending should make an impact. ALE

- Describe feelings rather than actions:

  As Nick walked dejectedly along the towpath near Chloe's house he hoped desperately that he might see her.

- Use another viewpoint:

  Chloe had seen Nick walking along the towpath near her house. It was not just by chance that she had been walking there too. She had seen him at the club and there he was on her doorstep. It was too good a chance to miss.

- Use the senses:

  The wind blew in Nick's face and the driving rain stung his cheeks. He thrust his hands deep into his pockets for warmth as he came in sight of Chloe's house.

- Set the scene:

  The canal looked greyer than usual today. Grim and grey. That was just how Nick felt as he trudged along the slippery towpath. But there did seem to be a tiny glimmer of sun.

Endings

Getting started is often difficult – but you will probably find that once you are over the first hurdle and the beginning is working, then writing the rest of the story is a bit easier. The difficulty is knowing how and when to stop.

The best written stories are the best planned stories. Many people start a story well, develop it in an interesting fashion but get too carried away. They begin to ramble and don't know how to finish. So they take the easy way out. Usually, stories like this end with a simple, disappointing and abrupt conclusion, such as:

> *It was all a dream.*
> *... and then I woke up.*
> *... and they lived happily ever after.*

So make sure your endings are planned and more interesting than those above!

Exercise 2

Look back at one of your previous stories and try some different beginnings.

Exercise 3

Look at the beginning of a story which you know well. Could you predict how the story might continue just from how it starts? Is it possible to guess at what the characters are going to be like from the way they are described early in the story?

RED ALERT RED ALERT RED ALERT RED

Instructions and explanations

Imagine trying to play a board game or load computer software using instructions which are vague, out of sequence and assume previous knowledge which you do not have. This might have happened to you – and it can be very frustrating. In giving or following instructions it is essential that you:

- give an accurate list of the materials, ingredients, tools and resources needed;
- give instructions in order – step by step;
- explain what to do briefly but accurately.

Exercise 1

Choose one of the following processes and write down instructions, following the stages given below:

Mending a puncture	Playing a simple game	Changing a plug
Making a sandwich	Sending an email	Making a paper aeroplane

Stage 1
List the main steps in the process. You could number them 1 to 8, for example.

Stage 2
Check that you have included each of the basic instructions. Now fill in some detail which will help to explain the process.

Stage 3
Try out your instructions on a friend. Be prepared to alter and improve the stages of your explanation to make them clearer, if necessary.

Exercise 2

These activities involve speaking and listening rather than writing, but still show the importance of explaining things clearly.

1   Try guiding a blindfolded partner safely around a room using only verbal instructions. Do not touch them. You must make sure that they do not walk into any furniture or other obstacles. Swap over and let your partner try giving you directions.

Giving instructions and explanations can be much more difficult than you might think. What you might consider a simple task may be very hard for someone who has never done it before. You must not assume that they automatically know and understand every term and expression you use. Imagine that they have arrived on earth from another planet – everything would be strange to them. Without insulting your reader or listener's intelligence, keep your instructions/explanations as clear as you can. Guide them step by step through the task. If you use special terms or expressions explain what they mean.

Exercise 2 continued

2   Sit back to back with a partner. You will each need a pencil and paper. You should draw a simple sketch then give your partner precise instructions for how to draw the sketch themselves.

How close is their sketch to yours?

Swap over and follow your partner's instructions to draw a different picture.

Exercise 3

As you know, it is vital to do each part of a task in the right order. Look at the tasks below. For each one, write down a sequence of events in the right order. You can make a list with bullet points, a flow chart or time line.

* How to boil an egg
* How to make a sandwich
* How to make a cup of tea or coffee
* How to send an email

Tactics

List resources needed.

Include step-by-step instructions.

Provide clear and detailed explanations.

RED ALERT RED ALERT

Letter writing

Understanding the jargon

Informal letters are those you write to people you know, for example friends and family.
Formal letters are those you write to people you don't know, for example companies.

Writing a letter enables you to communicate with someone many miles away who you perhaps have never met. Letters usually fall into two main categories: formal or informal.

The layout for both types of letter follows a definite pattern – although there are different views on this and the layout may vary occasionally.

Formal letters

Formal letters are kept as brief as possible. You need to explain clearly what you want so that no time is wasted with unnecessary or irrelevant details. You would write a formal, business letter to complain about something, to make a request or give important information.

Use plain, unlined white paper and black or blue ink. You may, of course, type or word process your letter. Always include your own address and that of the person you are writing to.

Exercise 1

Draft a letter to someone you knew at primary school – it could be a pupil or teacher – telling them how you are enjoying secondary school. In your planning, think about the way the two schools are different, what is new and strange to you and what you miss. If you choose to write to a pupil, you might give them some advice for when they start at secondary school. Remember to ask how they are so you will get a letter back. Here is a suggestion for how you could start.

> Dear Natasha,
>   I have been at St John's School for four weeks now and am beginning to find my way around. It all seemed very big and confusing when I first started here and my first day was pretty scary.

Choose the correct style, and make sure you organise your letter. ALE

Begin *Dear Sir or Madam* and end with *Yours faithfully*, if you do not know, or have not met the person you are writing to. If you do know them, use their name and end with *Yours sincerely* – taking care to spell it correctly. Never write your name above your address, in either formal or informal letters.

Informal letters

Informal (personal) letters are less serious in tone. How informal you make your letter will depend on the recipient (the person receiving the letter). For example, a letter to an older relative, while friendly in tone, would be different to one written to someone your own age. The content and the language need to be chosen carefully, with your reader in mind.

As with a formal letter, there is a recognised layout for informal letters. Here, however, the rules are more flexible. Whatever the task, here are some general guidelines.

- Include your address, but not that of the reader.

- Begin with their name, for example *Dear Uncle Dinesh ...*

- End informally, but in a way which suits your relationship with the person, for example *Love from, Best wishes, Yours sincerely*.

- Make sure that the letter is worth reading. Try to be as informative and interesting as you can. If possible, use questions to which your reader will respond and so write back to you.

- Take care that your style is lively – even chatty – but not sloppy or rambling. Your reader will soon lose interest.

Exercise 2

Now try drafting a formal letter using one of the ideas below. Remember the differences between the formal style of letter writing and the informal style.

- Accepting an invitation to a prize-giving presentation
- Asking an author to speak at your school Book Week
- A letter to the local newspaper complaining about the lack of facilities for young people

Tactics

Decide on your style of letter.

Put the address/es at the top.

Then the date.

Start *Dear ... .*

Finish appropriately.

RED ALERT RED ALERT RED ALERT RED

Writing to complain

It is often said that 'the pen is mightier than the sword' – which means that you can influence someone more effectively in writing than you can by force. The skill in using words to persuade another person to your point of view by thoughtful argument is a very useful one.

Read this letter carefully to see how the writer makes their point.

> 12 Barton Road
> Welmshaw
> Devon
> DN9 5ZX
> 24 February, 2000
>
> c/o The Amenities Department
> Welmshaw Council Offices
> 77 Drake Street
> Welmshaw, Devon
> DN7 8ZX
>
> Dear Sir / Madam,
> I wish to complain about the closure of the Youth Centre. I have attended the centre regularly for two years now. It is well equipped and carefully supervised. A wide range of activities is available, making Friday night the best part of my week.

Exercise 1

Imagine the standard of your school meals does not compare well with those at your primary school. Write a letter of complaint, suggesting improvements. You could begin like this:

> I have just started at this school and I have been very disappointed with the standard and variety of food offered in the school canteen.

Many of my friends also go to the centre on other nights as well. It gives them a place to relax and enjoy themselves with people of their own age.

My parents are happy for me to go to the centre because they know where I am and who I am with. They know that I am doing something useful rather than standing in the bus shelter in my spare time. The centre is also a safe place.

I can see that the Council needs to save money, but we all pay subs. This means that we cover the cost of the hall and have money left over for some equipment.

Isn't it better that we have somewhere to go? We don't drop litter in the street or cause trouble so the police are called.

Please think again about closing the centre. It gives us a brilliant time and we'll really miss it.

Yours faithfully

Tom Culverwell

This letter makes an impact because it is polite but thoughtful. The writer doesn't get angry, nor do they grovel. Notice how he starts by saying what the problem is and how it affects him:

• The writer starts with the first person singular, *I*.
• Next, he gives two supporting views from other people – his friends and his parents.
• Then he shows that he is thinking about the opposite side of the argument by saying that he understands how the Council might see the problem.
• Finally, he puts a question to the Council to make them think about the consequences of closing the Youth Centre. He ends by repeating his point in a polite way.

The Council would be unlikely to ignore a letter like this because it says what it has to say in a sensible manner and in a form which is easy to follow.

Exercise 2

Imagine you live in a village ten miles from the nearest town. There are only two bus services a day from the village to the town. Draft a letter of complaint to your local bus company, detailing your reasons and your suggestions for improvement. Include supporting facts and other people's opinions, for example:

> I live in the village of Molesworth and have for some time wondered why the number of daily bus services from Molesworth to Framtown could not be increased...

Tactics

Put your address at the top right of the letter.

Don't forget the date.

Add the company's address underneath on the left.

Order your information sensibly.

Finish your letter correctly.

Descriptive writing

Understanding the jargon

Bias is a strong opinion for or against an idea.

Part of the skill of a good writer is that they can make you believe in what they are saying. You are carried along by your imagination and you can picture the places and characters in your mind as if they were real. At the same time, the writer does not give too much information so that the pace, action or meaning of the story are spoiled.

Describing and creating characters

If you look around your classroom you will see many different faces and features. Some people may look quite alike but they are all individuals with different interests, attitudes and ideas. When describing any one person accurately and effectively, you need to notice those things which make him or her special.

There are many ways of describing characters, all of which should help you to build up a picture without seeming to give much information at all.

- Appearance   How someone looks is a good starting point – but avoid giving basic information which could apply to almost anyone. To say *he is tall* or *she has fair hair* could apply equally to a number of people. It is better to think about those things which make that individual unique. This is a good opportunity to use adjectives and adverbs to supply

Exercise 1

Read the two descriptions below. Both writers are talking about the same place, but from contrasting viewpoints. The descriptions show bias.

> The house stands in a very isolated position up a rough, unmade track. It is sadly neglected – the roof tiles are broken, the walls and ceilings need plastering and there is an urgent need for repairs to the drains. Inside most of the rooms there is evidence of rising damp. The whole property would benefit from complete redecoration and routine maintenance.

additional information. You might say *He is unusually tall for his age* or *Her light blonde hair contrasts sharply with her green eyes.*

- Behaviour   This does not refer to whether or not someone is always in trouble. It means how they move, stand or act which is different or special. By taking care with your word choice you can select verbs which most accurately reflect what you see. For example, *She drifted to the door and opened it lazily* or *He interrupted me – yet again – with another pointless remark* both give information to the reader more effectively than straightforward statements.

- Personality   It is sometimes difficult to separate behaviour and personality. Personality refers to whether a person is quiet and shy or lively and talkative.

- Background   The past history of a person may be relevant to your description. It is not normally necessary to give a complete biography, but where information helps to create a fuller picture it makes your character more real in the reader's imagination. You might say *She had been using the family computer almost since she could walk* or *Living up the long farm track, his walk to school takes him at least half an hour.*

- Describing places   The setting of a story is vitally important and is rather like preparing the stage before bringing on the actors. The tone and atmosphere of a story could hinge on your description. Imagine how you might portray the scene in a dentist's waiting room, a beach in summer, a busy marketplace or a teenager's bedroom. What you observe and choose to focus on could give exactly the right impression or quite the opposite to the one you intended.

Exercise 1 continued

This charming and unusual house enjoys a quiet position at the end of an idyllic country lane. Its period features and unashamed, old-world style make it ideal for restoration. After a small investment of time and money, its future owners would have a home of which they could be justly proud.

Try to describe one place from two opposing positions. You could write about your bedroom from your own viewpoint and balance it by saying how your parents feel about it. Another idea might be to use the view of a teacher and of a pupil about a classroom.

Tactics

Describe appearance, behaviour, personality, background.

Describe places.

69

For and against

There are times when you are asked to express your feelings and give a point of view. To make a good case you will need to have thought about the issue carefully beforehand and have found evidence and examples to support what you are saying. In the same way that you would not accuse someone of a crime without evidence to back you up, any argument you are presenting needs to be supported by reliable sources of information to be convincing.

The boxes below and on page 71 show some of the arguments for and against vegetarianism.

For

Animal welfare: cruelty – taken long distances to be killed. Some kept in poor or cramped conditions, e.g. pigs, veal calves, battery hens. Live short, unnatural lives. Wild animals – better lives.

Humans do not need meat to survive.

Some animal products are not good for humans, e.g. fat, etc.

Grain fed to animals could feed people – export to poor countries.

Alternative, non-animal products could be used.

Animal diseases – passed to humans?

Exercise 1

1   Add some ideas of your own to either one or both sides of the table above.
2   Choose one side. Think about where you might find further information about that side of the argument.
3   How would you write your views down? Which part of your notes would make a good starting point? How would you make a strong case and a convincing conclusion?

> Vegetarianism is the only option for intelligent people in today's society. I have been a vegetarian for two years now and would urge anyone to make the same decision for themselves, and here's why...

Against

Animals are killed quickly and painlessly.

Rearing and producing animals – income for farmers.

Animals provide food and other things, e.g. leather, fertiliser.

Meat tastes good! Burgers, etc.

Animals graze areas which can't be used for anything else.

Environmental issues?

Farm animals – not pets.

Cows need to breed to give milk.

Animals kept until old and useless?

If you were asked to write an essay about the subject of vegetarianism, rather than argue a case for or against, then you would use points from each column – you would not need to agree with one side or the other. Having explored the subject you are providing the reader with balanced information – then it is up to them to make up their own mind. This would be an open-ended essay.

Exercise 2

Draw up a 'For and Against' list for an issue about which you feel strongly.

• Should 12-year-olds be expected to buy their own clothes?
• private medicine
• weekly or monthly pocket money

71

Handling speech

In your writing, you will probably include the words a person actually says, especially in a story. You will already know that this is called speech or dialogue. There are two types of speech:

• direct speech which tells you exactly what someone says;
• indirect or reported speech which is what someone might say if they were listening to other people talking, but were not part of the conversation.

Imagine that a conversation is taking place and that what each person is saying is contained in a speech bubble.

To punctuate this as a piece of direct speech, you must be aware of two main rules:

• Always use a new line for each new speaker.
• Start and end each piece of speech with inverted commas.

Example

"Are you going skating tonight, Will?" asked Danny.
    "Yeah. What time have we got to meet?"
    "Um ... dunno. Think it's about seven."
    "Do you want a lift? My mum is taking me. She could take you if you like."
    "Okay, but she might not have room. Shouldn't you ask her first?"
    "Suppose so. I'll ring you when I get home."

Exercise 1

1 Draw a simple cartoon with a speech bubble conversation.
2 Write down the same conversation as direct speech using inverted commas.
3 Rewrite the conversation as reported (indirect) speech (remove all the inverted commas).

Example
1.

Apart from the words which the writer has put in to help the piece make sense, all these words have been said in turn by the two speakers. Each 'turn' has a set of inverted commas (or speech marks) around it.

Long sections of speech can be a bit boring – the reader can feel left out. You will also notice that the speech itself is rather sloppy. It includes some unnecessary words, hesitation and slang.

The entire speech could be summed up and written as indirect or reported speech much more effectively.

> ## Example
>
> Danny asked Will if he was going skating. Will was going and asked what time they had to meet. Danny thought it was at seven o'clock. Will offered his friend a lift, providing he had time to check with his mother first. They agreed to confirm the arrangement later that day.

This text still contains all the information but without the speech. The meaning is the same but it is written more plainly.

The spoken and the written word

It is very important, when you are writing, that you do not write as you speak. When you speak you may use careless words, phrases or expressions – but, because you are speaking, you can correct yourself as you go. You are not able to do that when you are writing. The final draft of your work is there for everyone to see. The words you speak are gone once you have said them: the words you write may stay forever!

Exercise 1 continued

2. "Julie, what time is the film on?" asked Seema.
   "I don't know, Seema. Call the cinema," replied Julie.

3. Seema asked Julie what time the film was on. Julie didn't know and suggested Seema phoned the cinema.

Preparing for the optional tests

- It is very difficult to revise for an English test – but you **can** prepare for it.

- Don't leave your preparation until the night before the test. Start thinking about the test and the points covered on the sheet well in advance.

- There are two tests, one on reading and one on writing. In each test you will be given 15 minutes to read the material and 60 minutes to do the work.

- **The reading test** You will be given three or four pieces to read; they might be poems, passages from non–fiction books or extracts from stories. You need to show that you can read a variety of texts and understand them clearly. In the questions you may be asked to give the meanings of different words and phrases, search for information or use what you have found out to draw your own conclusions.

- **The writing test** There will probably be a short test and then a longer test. There will be clear instructions about what you have to do. For example, you may be told that the test expects you to write in a way that will persuade, inform, explain, entertain or instruct your reader. These are directions which you must take notice of and follow. All the writing skills which you have learned must be used with thought and care. You will need to write in a way which fits the purpose and the audience it is aimed at.

Some general tips

- **Read the paper very carefully**   It sounds obvious, but you would be surprised how many people don't. Read passages at least twice. Read questions and do what they say. If you are asked for a list, then write a list. If a question is worth six marks make certain you give more information than for the one worth two marks.

- **Keep an eye on the time**   You probably won't have had much experience of writing 'against the clock'. Don't spend too much time on any one question. Move on. Make sure that you give yourself time to check your work. If you seem to have finished early, look back at your work – you may have missed something or not written enough.

- **Check**   You must plan your work – you may be given marks if your planning shows what you were going to write, even if you do not have time to write it. Check your spelling, punctuation and paragraphs. Check your choice of words, vocabulary and expression.

- **Reading**   Review your personal reading. Look at your reading diary. Look at some types of reading which you would not normally consider. Do you know the difference between fiction and non-fiction? Fact and opinion? What does *genre* mean?

- **Writing**   Look at the comments on work you have done – follow up on any mistakes you tend to make. Check any problems with your teacher or look at the relevant section in this book.

- **Handwriting**   Is your writing clear? In a test you have to write quickly. Is the writing you do when you are in a hurry still easy to read?

- **Spelling**   Make a list of words which you keep getting wrong. Double-check you can spell words which you have heard or have used in English lessons. In the test, make certain that any words on the paper have the correct spelling if you use them in your answers.

- **Punctuation**   When you check your work at the end of the test, try to read it as if you were seeing it for the first time. Take a short breath for each comma and a longer one for a full stop. Can you read what you have written without gasping for breath?

- **And finally, good luck!**

Giving a talk

You are almost certain to be asked to speak to your class at some stage in Year 7. It may be to review a book you have read, to report on some research you have done or to talk about a subject in the role of 'expert'. Even though this is not a very formal situation and you will know everyone in the room, you might still feel nervous. It is quite natural for you to feel worried but do remember that everyone else is sure to feel the same.

With good preparation and enough practice you will find that you are confident when it comes to your turn. Here are some ideas to help you prepare and present your talk.

- **Prepare** As with all planning, brainstorm your ideas on a sheet of paper. Do not write everything out in full sentences – it is not necessary.

- **Think** Consider the purpose of your talk – to interest, inform and even entertain your audience. The audience will all be of your own age, so what appeals to you will appeal to them if you select your material carefully.

- **Order** Pick out the main points from your brainstorm and put them on another piece of paper in the form of a flow chart or list. Next, on pieces of paper or, better still, postcards, write out the order of your talk in note form.

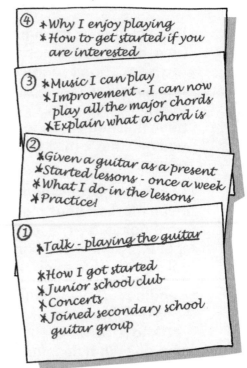

④ * Why I enjoy playing
* How to get started if you are interested

③ * Music I can play
* Improvement - I can now play all the major chords
* Explain what a chord is

② * Given a guitar as a present
* Started lessons - once a week
* What I do in the lessons
* Practice!

① * Talk - playing the guitar
* How I got started
* Junior school club
* Concerts
* Joined secondary school guitar group

Exercise 1

I   Prepare a talk (lasting one minute) on any subject. Make very brief notes on the most interesting aspects as if you were going to give the talk to a friend or relative, like the example below.

> Talk on yoga
> - originates in India
> - good for flexibility, digestion and stress
> - different positions
> - different types of yoga
> - famous people who do yoga

- **Number your cards**   It is difficult to avoid the temptation to write everything down – sadly, this will mean that you end up reading to the class instead of talking to them.

- **Rehearse**   Once you are satisfied with what you have planned, practise it at home. Use a quiet room. Repeat the talk to yourself – then try it aloud in front of a mirror. Explain to your family what you are doing. Only perform it for them when you are ready.

- **Time yourself**   Make sure that you have enough information to last the time available.

- **Delivery**   This simply means, giving the talk. When it comes to your turn, try to look at your audience. If you can, put some expression into your voice – don't say everything in the same tone. Look around the room to check that the class are following what you are saying. If they are paying attention and keeping eye contact then you are doing well. You will know if they are bored!

- **Speak up: slow down**   Many people, when speaking publicly, speak too fast and too quietly. Try to talk at two-thirds of your normal speed. Also, try to direct your voice to the back of the room, not down into your notes.

- **Smile**   Try to smile at your audience and look cheerful – even if you don't feel it. Actors, politicians, lawyers and anyone who speaks in public gets nervous. Calm down. Breathe deeply. Keep still. If necessary use a clipboard for your notes, but do not hide behind it.

- **Afterwards**   Good planning will mean that you have thought about the sort of questions that the class might ask you. You will be able to handle them easily. When it is all over, think what you have learned from the experience and how you could improve in future.

Exercise 2

If possible, tape record your talk, imagining you are in front of an audience as you speak. Play it back to yourself. How do you sound? Are you talking too quickly or too slowly? Are you speaking clearly? Does the talk flow well? Does it make sense?

If you can see areas you can improve, re-record yourself, bearing those improvements in mind. Does the second recording sound better?

Tactics

Prepare well.

Order your information.

Practise your talk.

Speak loudly and clearly.

RED ALERT RED ALERT RED ALERT RED AL

Writing a script

Understanding the jargon

A set is the scenery and other props that show a play's setting.
Props or properties are the smaller articles needed on stage, for example lamps, cutlery.
The narrator is the person in the play who tells the audience what is happening between the action.

Plays are always written as scripts. Unlike prose (which is written in sentences and paragraphs) or poetry (in lines and stanzas), plays are written in acts and scenes. There might be several acts, each made up of a number of scenes – or there might be just one act.

A script tells the actors what to say – their parts. The narrator gives information about how the characters should speak or move. There is also information to help the person organising the play (the producer or director) to decide on the set and properties which will be needed. The narrator's words are not spoken as part of the play!

To get a better idea of what a script looks like, switch on an episode of a television series. Turn the volume right down and select subtitles. The words being spoken by each actor will appear on screen in a different colour. Other information about the action is also given – this is the narration.

Exercise 1

1   On a large sheet of paper, sketch out ideas for different scenes.
2   Say where each takes place and what happens.
3   Use stick figures and brief notes to explain what you mean (like those shown on page 79).
4   You will end up with a storyboard – you might have used one before.
    Your storyboard will help you to write the play as a full script.
5   The storyboard given on page 79 is just a suggestion. You will almost certainly have changed the names, places and characters. Try to give your version a different ending.
6   When you write your play, do not forget to give the actors some help. Remember that you are the playwright and have to write everything – parts and stage directions.

Tactics

Write a play in acts and scenes.

Describe the set.

Add stage directions.

Write a script for each character's part.

Add a narrator, if needed.

Plays are written in acts and scenes, with scripts for the actors' parts. ALE

Here is the first scene of a one-act play called *Just Helping Out*. Eventually (perhaps after many changes) all six scenes will be written by you!

Act I Scene I

The scene is an ordinary kitchen, anywhere, at 8am. Emma and her younger brother, Tim, are sitting in surly silence over breakfast. It is a school day, but neither seems in a hurry. Tim is tapping his spoon repeatedly on an empty bowl and staring blankly at the table.

Emma   Do you have to do that?

Tim   What? (*barely taking notice of his sister*)

Emma   Use that spoon like a drumstick.

Tim   Why not?

Emma   It's irritating.

Tim   (*defensively*) Better to be irritating than embarrassing. Anyway, fancy you volunteering to help with the play – and in assembly too.

Emma   It'll be fun. Besides, I like doing things for school.

Tim   I don't. School's just work.

Emma   So is the basketball team work? You're in that. And the computer club and …

Tim   (*interrupting hastily, but now with a smile on his face*) Okay. Take your point.

A voice from another room shouts "The bus is here!"

What might happen next? How could the play continue in the remaining five scenes?

Exercise 1 continued

1

Emma and Tim – talk over breakfast

2

Emma's friend gets her to help with the play – behind the scenes

3

Emma enjoys helping with the lighting

4

Someone drops out of the play

5

A teacher asks Emma to take the part

6

Emma's brilliant performance!

79

Speak up: speak out

The largest section in this book is on writing – and the smallest is on speaking and listening. This might seem rather odd, because we spend much more of our time communicating by speaking than by any other means. You have been using speech for at least ten years – but you have probably only been able to write anything that someone could understand for about seven of those years. You must be really good at speaking by now!

Speaking and listening at school is a bit different. It does not mean just having a chat. In your English sessions (and elsewhere) you are speaking with a purpose. Notice that this paragraph begins with the words Speaking *and* listening not Speaking *or* listening. In your lessons, you will be expected to take part. This is important because, further up the school, in Year 11, you will be assessed (as part of your GCSE course) on your *oral* ability. That is, on how you speak *and* listen. It would be a good idea to get some practice! Here are some ground rules to help you.

- Understand the task   Whether you are working in pairs, or in a larger group, you need to be sure what your task involves. You may be asked to solve a problem, prepare a presentation or discuss a poem. Check that you know what the eventual outcome will be – and stick to it.

- Share the work   In any group, there are different jobs to do. Someone needs to take notes on what you discuss. Someone needs to be in charge. Someone must report back to the class at the end of the session. All these jobs need to be done and it shouldn't be the same person all the time. Try to give everyone a turn.

- Listen   If everyone tends to talk at once, let the chosen leader of the group decide who speaks and when. If this causes problems, use a special object which gives a person permission to speak. In William Golding's *Lord of the Flies* a conch shell was used, and anyone

Exercise 1

Try 'The Balloon Debate'. Imagine that you and your group are in a hot air balloon. It is heading towards a mountain side. In order to save everyone else, someone must parachute out of the balloon. The pilot must stay, but who should jump? Number each of the passengers, then pick a number at random. Argue the case for that passenger to stay. You may find that you are arguing for someone who you do not think should stay – this is called 'playing devil's advocate' – you are just arguing to get the discussion going. You can decide on your own passengers, but here are a few ideas to get you started:

- a top cancer surgeon
- a grandmother
- you

- a popular musician
- a promising student
- a charity worker

holding it had permission to speak. Use something (a pencil case or a ruler, for example) like a relay baton. Pass it from person to person. Only the person holding the object can speak. *Everyone* must respect this rule.

- Work together You will, at some time, be asked to work with people who you do not know very well or who are not your friends. Get used to it! There are millions of people in the world who you have not met – you might end up working with any one of them. Don't think of them as strangers – but new friends. Think about how you could encourage a shy person to take part. How you could help someone who is not very confident to share their ideas? How would you make a more talkative member of the group listen to another person's point of view? Try these ideas.

Examples

"I think that is a good idea. What do you think, Evie?"
"I think that it is a good point – but I am not sure that Dermot would agree."

Avoid asking questions which will only get a *yes* or *no* answer. These are called closed questions.

An open question gets a better response:

Examples

"Do you like this poem?"
"No."

Examples

"What do you think is the best line in this poem?"
"Well, I liked the part where ... "

Exercise 2

Choose a scene from a favourite play, or find an extract in a book that has lots of dialogue. Practise reading the passage aloud, using lots of expression and trying to adopt a different 'voice' for each character.

81

TEST PAPER 1

There are two parts to this test: reading and writing.

Reading

There are three pieces to read in this section:

    a The poem 'Leisure' by W H Davies

    b The poem 'The Listeners' by Walter de la Mare

    c A non-fiction extract called *The Sixth Sense*.

Spend 15 minutes reading the poems, passage and questions – but do not write anything yet. Answer all the questions in this section. You should be able to complete the test in one hour.

Leisure

What is this life, if full of care,
We have no time to stand and stare?

No time to stand beneath the boughs
And stare as long as sheep and cows;

No time to see, when woods we pass,
Where squirrels hide their nuts in grass;

No time to see, in broad daylight,
Streams full of stars, like skies at night;

No time to turn at Beauty's glance,
And watch her feet, how they can dance;

No time to wait till her mouth can
Enrich that smile her eyes began?

A poor life this if, full of care,
We have no time to stand and stare.

W H Davies

---

1   Give another word or phrase of your own for:

    a leisure (as in the poem's title)

    _____

    b care (line one)

    _____

2   Using the exact words of the poem, write two things which the poet likes to look at.

    _____

3   **a** What type of places does the poet seem to like?

    _____

    b What does this tell us about him?

    _____

The Listeners

"Is there anybody there?" said the Traveller,
    Knocking on the moonlit door;
And his horse in the silence champed the grasses
    Of the forest's ferny floor;
And a bird flew up out of the turret,
    Above the Traveller's head:
And he smote upon the door again a second time;
    "Is there anybody there?" he said.
But no one descended to the Traveller;
    No head from the leaf-fringed sill
Leaned over and looked into his grey eyes,
    Where he stood perplexed and still.
But only a host of phantom listeners
    That dwelt in the lone house then
Stood listening in the quiet of the moonlight
    To that voice from the world of men:
Stood thronging the faint moonbeams on the dark stair,
    That goes down to the empty hall,
Hearkening in an air stirred and shaken
    By the lonely Traveller's call.
And he felt in his heart their strangeness,
    Their stillness answering his cry,
While his horse moved, cropping the dark turf,
    'Neath the starred and leafy sky;
For he suddenly smote on the door, even
    Louder, and lifted his head –
"Tell them I came, and no one answered,
    That I kept my word," he said.
Never the least stir made the listeners,
    Though every word he spake
Fell echoing through the shadowiness of the still house
    From the one man left awake:
Ay, they heard his foot upon the stirrup,
    And the sound of iron on stone,
And how the silence surged softly backward,
    When the plunging hoofs were gone.

Walter de la Mare

4 The poet has used alliteration in this poem. He repeats consonant letter

sounds close together. Write an example below. (Use the poet's

exact words.)

✎ _____

5 Here is a list of things which happen in the poem, but they are in the wrong order.

Write down the correct order, using just the letter of each stage.

a No one answers.

d He rides away.

b He shouts that he kept his word.

e He knocks again.

c The horseman knocks on the door.

✎ _____

6 The man in the poem says '*I kept my word*', meaning he had kept a promise. Write three to four sentences saying what his promise might have been.

✎ _____

_____

_____

7 Who do you think *the listeners* could have been?

✎ _____

The Sixth Sense

I have known for a long time that my dogs are clever, but I still find it hard to believe. They have powers which no scientist or inventor could match. The most elaborate and expensive radar equipment is pitiful when compared to the natural abilities of these humble canines.

Human beings are clever; they can communicate, invent, create and design. They use their five senses – but in a quite limited way. Like the radar of a nuclear submarine or the detection systems of a spy plane, we can hear and see. But we can also touch, taste and smell in a way that they cannot.

Even these senses are sometimes ignored in the bustle of everyday living. A person who is blind becomes much more sensitive than any sighted person to sound, touch, taste and smell. But my dogs can do even better than that. They can sense, almost instinctively, when I am going to take them for a walk. They can tell when someone is angry or upset. They will go to the front door to greet my wife, long before her car turns into the drive. They have a sixth sense, which even the most advanced equipment could not hope to copy.

8 List the five senses:

✎ _____

9 Give another word or phrase of your own for:

a humble   **b** sensitive   **c** instinctively

✎ _____   ✎ _____   ✎ _____

10 Which of these five points is the main point of the passage?

Write the correct sentence.

- Dogs are clever.
- Humans do not use their senses enough.
- Modern technology is not very good.
- Dogs have an ability that cannot be copied.
- Blind people hear better than people with sight.

✎ _____

Writing

This writing test asks you to describe, interest and entertain your reader.

- The first task is a short one to help with your planning. (15 minutes)
- The second task is the main task. (45 minutes)

Task 1

Think of an interesting place or a lively scene which you could describe. It might be a busy town or a market on a Saturday morning – or a quiet spot in the country. Choose a place you know well. List ten things which you can see or hear in the place you have chosen. (You will be using these when you come to Task 2.)

✎ _____

_____

_____

_____

_____

Task 2

Write a description of the place you have chosen. Use sentences and paragraphs. Check your spelling and punctuation when you have finished.

✎ _____

_____

_____

_____

_____

There are two parts to this test: reading and writing.

Reading

There are three pieces to read in this section:

    a   The poem 'Timothy Winters' by Charles Causley

    b An extract from *Cider with Rosie* by Laurie Lee

    c An extract from a brochure about Greenacres School.

Spend 15 minutes reading the poems, passage and questions – but do not write anything yet. Answer all the questions in this section. You should be able to complete the test in one hour.

Timothy Winters

Timothy Winters comes to school
With eyes as wide as a football pool,
Ears like bombs and teeth like splinters:
A blitz of a boy is Timothy Winters.

His belly is white, his neck is dark,
And his hair is an exclamation mark.
His clothes are enough to scare a crow
And through his britches the blue
    winds blow.

When teacher talks he won't hear
    a word
And he shoots down dead the
    arithmetic-bird,
He licks the patterns off his plate
And he's not even heard of the
    Welfare State.

Timothy Winters has bloody feet
And he lives in a house on Suez Street,
He sleeps in a sack on the kitchen floor
And they say there aren't boys like him
    any more.

Old Man Winters likes his beer
And his missus ran off with a
    bombardier,
Grandma sits in the grate with a gin
And Timothy's dosed with an aspirin.

The Welfare Worker lies awake
But the law's as tricky as a ten-foot
    snake,
So Timothy Winters drinks his cup
And slowly goes on growing up.

At Morning Prayers the Headmaster
    helves
For children less fortunate than
    ourselves,
And the loudest response in the room
    is when
Timothy Winters roars "Amen!"

So come one angel, come on ten:
Timothy Winters says "Amen"
Amen amen amen amen.
Timothy Winters, Lord.

                       Amen

Charles Causley

I   Give five facts about Timothy which make you feel sorry for him.

_____

_____

_____

2 What do you think the poet means by a *blitz of a boy*?

✎ _____

_____

_____

3 The words *as* and *like* often show that a simile is being used. Find two examples from the poem and write them down.

✎ _____

_____

_____

4 Reread the first two lines of the third verse. What do they tell you about Timothy's attitude towards school? Answer in at least two sentences.

✎ _____

_____

_____

5 The Headmaster asks the children to pray for those less fortunate than ourselves.

a Why is Timothy's response the loudest?

✎ _____

_____

_____

b What does his reaction tell you about him?

✎ _____

_____

_____

From **Cider with Rosie**

The village school at that time provided all the instruction we were likely to ask for. It was a small stone barn divided by a wooden partition into two rooms – The Infants and The Big Ones. There was one dame teacher, and perhaps a young girl assistant. Every child in the valley crowding there, remained till he was fourteen years old, then was presented to the working field or factory with nothing in his head more burdensome than a few mnemonics, a jumbled list of wars, and a dreamy image of the world's geography. It seemed enough to get by with, in any case; and was one up on our poor old grandparents.

Laurie Lee

6   Give another word or phrase of your own for:

   a   partition (line 2)

✎ _____

   b   image (line 7)

✎ _____

7   Give two examples from the passage of things Laurie Lee learned at school. Use the writer's exact words.

✎ _____

_____

_____

8   What jobs might the children have done after they left the school?

✎ _____

_____

_____

9   Why do you think that the education given at the school was enough to get by with?

✎ _____

_____

_____

Greenacres Community School

Greenacres is an 11–16 secondary school with, at present, 800 students. Opened in 1990, the campus is set in five hectares of sports fields and boasts purpose-built accommodation of modern and practical design.

The newly constructed Brocton Building houses a language laboratory and drama complex while the nearby Stanway Centre offers indoor sports and leisure facilities to the whole community. These include a pre-school playgroup and senior citizens club during the day and classes on everything from fencing to folk art in the evening. An additional squash court has been completed only last week and is already proving popular.

We believe that any student at Greenacres will receive a top class education. A recent report praised the 'broad and varied curriculum' on offer here. Local colleges and employers often comment on the confidence and maturity of our ex-students – as well as on their impressive academic records.

Greenacres – making the students of today into the citizens of tomorrow.

10 Give two examples of new things at the school.

✎ _____

11 **a** Give two facts about the school.

✎ _____

b Give an example of an opinion using the exact words of the passage.

✎ _____

12 Why have the words *broad and varied curriculum* been put in inverted commas in the passage?

✎ _____

Writing

These writing tests ask you to inform, persuade and advise your reader.

- The first task is a short one. (15 minutes)
- The second task is the main task. (45 minutes)

Task 1

Write one paragraph for a school brochure which would inform parents and persuade them that they should send their son or daughter to your school. Note down some facts about your school which you feel are good selling points.

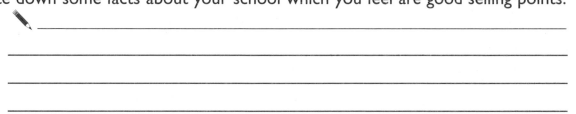

✎ _____

_____

_____

_____

Task 2

On spare paper write an article to inform and advise Year 6 pupils who will be starting at your school next September. Do not use the names of staff or other students. Use these ideas to help you with your planning:

- Comment on equipment which they will find useful.
- What is different about secondary school?
- What things are difficult to get used to?
- How did you feel before you started the school?

Answers to exercises

Singulars and plurals
Exercise 1
knives flies deer calves halves women
stadiums or stadia octopuses radii

Wordfinder
Exercise 1
rat nit man pig rat dog hare swift
owl ant cat

Exercise 2
technology: no, log
handkerchief: an, and, hand, chief
disgust: is, gust
wolfish: wolf, fish, is   slippery: slip, per, lip
trowel: row   flour: our   definitely: definite,
finite, fin, it, nit   intelligent: in, tell, gent
awkward: ward   hospital: pit, it
shepherd: she, he, herd, her

Common errors
Exercise 1
1 two, to, too
2 too, to
3 to, two, too

Exercise 2
1 their, there
2 their, their
3 they're, their

Exercise 3
1 hear, here
2 here, hear
3 here, hear

Exercise 4
1 our, are, hour
2 hour, are
3 our, hour

Sentences
Exercise 1
1 going
2 sat
3 cried

Exercise 2
1 Lindsay
2 the team
3 the teacher

Exercise 3
1 Sarah
2 the garden
3 a headache
4 the dog
5 the film
6 the sandwich

Exercise 4
1 phrase
2 sentence
3 sentence
4 phrase
5 sentence
6 phrase
7 phrase
8 sentence

Capital letters

Mrs Carter shouted upstairs to her two children, Ben and Kate. It was Tuesday morning and they had to be in Birmingham to meet the train from London.

"I just want to hear the end of this Beatles' song," Kate yelled back. Ben grabbed his new Nike jacket off the landing before racing downstairs.

Nouns

Exercise 1

cards, flowers, sheep, cattle, people

Exercise 2

school (or shoal), litter, troop, sleuth, murder

Punctuation

1 His lunch consisted of an apple, chocolate biscuit and three cheese sandwiches.
2 "Run quickly!" shouted Seema. "The tide is coming in!"
3 Sadly, the injured blackbird died from its injuries. (*Its* does not need any punctuation because it does not mean 'it is'.)
4 "Stay where you are!" bellowed the firefighter.
5 "Gemma, I've found your trainers; they were under your bed all the time!"

Connectives

Exercise 1

Some examples are:

1 while
2 during
3 eventually or finally

Exercise 2

1 on the other hand
2 although
3 causing
4 eventually

Apostrophes

Exercise 1

hasn't, couldn't, I'll, she'd, didn't

Exercise 2

1 the boy's trainers
2 the captain's decisions
3 the team's results
4 a day's work
5 all the dogs' tails

Genre

Exercise 1

1 science fiction
2 ghost story
3 romance

ANSWERS

Answers to test papers

With many questions in English, there is more than one 'right' answer. Here are some suggested answers. Use a dictionary or ask your teacher for help if you think your answer is wrong – it may not be.

Test paper 1

Reading

1 **a** leisure – spare time, time to relax, a time when you are not working

   b care – trouble, worry

2 where squirrels hide their nuts in grass, streams full of stars

3 **a** The poet likes fields and woods, both of which are found in the country.

   b He likes country places, so we could say that he enjoys peace and quiet. The whole poem is saying that we are so busy that we have no time to look at things or think about what is going on around us.

4 the forest's ferny floor, the silence surged softly

5 c, a, e, b, d

6 His promise was that he would come to the house. It seems that he was supposed to meet someone. The house was empty. Whoever he was meant to meet had not turned up.

7 The listeners could have been ghosts. They might have been echoes or just the horseman's imagination. They may also have been the spirits of people who had lived there in the past.

8 sight, sound, touch, taste and smell

9 **a** humble – ordinary, unsophisticated, common

   b sensitive – is aware of, notices

   c instinctively – knows/feels without being told

10 Dogs have an ability that cannot be copied.

Test paper 2

Reading

1 You might mention that he has bloody feet or that he sleeps in a sack on the kitchen floor. He licks the patterns off his plate so he is probably often hungry. His clothes are ragged because through his britches the blue winds blow. Also his neck is dark – so he is not very clean. Several times his family is mentioned and they do not appear to care for him, apart from giving him aspirin.

2 Blitz was a term used in World War II to describe the bombing. If you have said anything which describes Timothy as shocking or alarming, you are close to the answer.

3 ears like bombs, teeth like splinters, the law's as tricky as a ten-foot snake

4 Timothy is not interested in school. He does not listen to the teacher. He does not like maths.

5 **a** He wants to pray for people who are less fortunate than he is despite having a poor life himself.

   b This tells us that, for all his own misfortune, he is kind.

6 **a** partition – a division across the room

   b image – picture or idea

7 the world's geography, a list of wars, a few mnemonics

8 They might work in the field (farming) or in a factory.

9 They did not need much education because of the work they were going to do.

10 The Brocton building – and therefore the language laboratory and drama complex; the additional squash court

11 **a** You should have noted anything for which there is obvious evidence, for example the buildings, field etc.

   b We believe ... is an opinion – it has no real evidence to support it.

12 These words are in inverted commas because they are said by someone else. They are given as a quotation.

Antonym	word meaning the opposite to another word
Assonance	repetition of vowel sounds
Bias	giving only one view or one side of an argument
Cliché	a phrase or expression which is over-used
Context	looking at a word within a sentence, or looking at a text and thinking about when it was written (the social and historical background), to help understand the meaning more fully
Criticism	saying what is good and bad about a book, poem or play, and why
Essay	a piece of writing (usually factual) on a subject from a range of viewpoints. An essay may come to a definite conclusion or it might just investigate different, opposing ideas.
Form	the shape or pattern of a piece of writing
Formal	speaking or writing in a serious way
Image	a picture or idea in the mind, or in the imagination
Informal	speaking or writing which is casual or light-hearted
Metaphor	making a comparison between two things as if one of them had changed in shape or form to resemble something else
Mnemonic	a group of words (which may or may not make sense), used to help remember something, for example the mnemonic Every Good Boy Deserves Favour could help you remember musical scales EGBDF
Personification	describing something in human terms or as having human qualities. Tennyson's poem 'The Eagle' describes the bird as clasping the cliff with crooked hands.

Props/properties   objects used by actors in a play

Quotation   the actual words which a person says, usually shown in inverted commas or italic type. In a text, words are put in inverted commas to show that they are not the writer's own.

Rhyme scheme   the pattern of rhyme in a poem. Each line is given a letter of the alphabet. The first line becomes a and any other lines which rhyme with that are also called a. If the next line does not rhyme with the first it is called b. A poem with lines one and two rhyming together and lines three and four rhyming would have a rhyme scheme of a a b b.

Rhythm   the pattern of 'beats' in a line. Different combinations of strong and weak beats give definite and recognisable patterns.

Standard English   the most widely used and commonly understood version of spoken or written English

Stanza   a group of lines in poetry, also known as a verse

Simile   making a comparison, often using the words *as* or *like*, for example *as quick as lightning*

Synonym   a word having the same meaning as another

Verse   a group of lines in poetry

INDEX